THE BATHROOM
IDEA BOOK

THE BATHROOM
IDEA BOOK

Andrew Wormer

The Taunton Press

For Anne, and for Annie

Taunton
BOOKS & VIDEOS
for fellow enthusiasts

Printed in the United States of America
10 9 8 7 6 5 4 3 2

The Bathroom Idea Book was originally published in hardcover
in 1999 by The Taunton Press, Inc.

The Taunton Press, Inc., 63 South Main Street, PO Box 5506, Newtown, CT 06470-5506
e-mail: tp@taunton.com

Distributed by Publishers Group West

TITLE PAGE PHOTO
Jeremy Samuelson

DEDICATION PHOTO
Brian Vanden Brink

CONTENTS PHOTOS (left to right)
Andrew Wormer, David Duncan Livingston, Tim Street-Porter, Brian Vanden Brink,
courtesy Formica, courtesy *Fine Homebuilding* magazine (© The Taunton Press),
Tim Street-Porter

INTRODUCTION PHOTOS
Carolyn L. Bates (p. 2), Roger Turk/Northlight Photography (p. 3), Tim Street-Porter
(p. 4, top), Carolyn L. Bates (p. 4, bottom), Carolyn L. Bates (p. 5)

COLOPHON PHOTO
Grey Crawford

Library of Congress Cataloging-in Publication Data

Wormer, Andrew.
    The bathroom idea book / Andrew Wormer.
      p. cm.
    ISBN 1-56158-313-8 hardcover
    ISBN 1-56158-394-4 paperback
    1. Bathrooms—Remodeling. I. Title.
TH4816.W67   1999
747.7'8—dc21   99-21103
                                   CIP

ACKNOWLEDGMENTS

I used to think that building bathrooms was an involved process until I started writing about them...talk about longing for the good old days. Fortunately, I've been able to rely on literally hundreds of people in the writing of this book.

In most cases, I've spoken directly with the architects and designers involved in each of the projects shown in this book. They've all been extremely helpful in explaining their ideas, supplying information about materials and fixtures, and offering general design advice. Wherever possible, their names and addresses have been included in the credits listed in the back of the book. I also received considerable help from the National Kitchen and Bath Association (NKBA); thanks especially to Michelle Morgan and Rhonda Moritz there. I encourage anyone considering a new bathroom to contact any of these talented folks.

In some cases, I've also spoken to the tradespeople involved in these projects. As a builder myself, I don't think that the general contractors, carpenters, plumbers, electricians, tile-setters, painters, and other professionals who actually build bathrooms get nearly enough credit. So for those both known (in which case you've been credited) and unknown, my hat is off to your skills and professionalism.

Many manufacturers have also had a hand in this book, either by supplying photographs or information and advice about their products. You'll find them listed under *For More Information* at the back of the book.

As a former editor at *Fine Homebuilding* magazine, I've tried my hand at professional bathroom photography. Believe me, it isn't easy: too many mirrors and not enough room. That's why I admire so much the work of the photographers who have contributed to this book. They've been invaluable, both for the photos they've

taken and for the information about designers they've been able to give me. They too are listed in the credits.

And while my grumbling during the writing and editing process may have convinced them otherwise, I really appreciate the opportunity to work again with the talented folks at The Taunton Press. Steve Culpepper, the acquisitions editor there, has been a long-time colleague from *Fine Homebuilding* days and a good friend. The book's designer, Henry Roth, has worked magic, transmogrifying one outline, hundreds of photos, and thousands of words into something that is considerably more than the sum of its parts. The behind-the-scenes staff—Carolyn Mandarano and Peter Chapman, in particular—have been largely responsible for transforming the idea of this book into a reality. And at the eye of the storm has been Carol Kasper, who has had to be the grease to all of the squeaky wheels involved in this project.

Whether editing text, finding photos, tracking down names, or reminding me about deadlines, she has been the one who has kept this book on track.

Some of the photos in this book were shot by either current or former members of the *Fine Homebuilding* staff. Thanks once again to editor Kevin Ireton and the rest of the people there—friends all—for making its considerable resources available during the writing of this book.

And as anyone who has written a book knows, family members, friends, and colleagues sometimes get ignored unintentionally during the writing process. To them, both my apologies and my heartfelt thanks for your support. It will be great to be back among the living. Finally, my love and thanks to Anne and my children Sam and Anna; the next great bathroom belongs to you guys!

CONTENTS

INTRODUCTION

The average family bathroom is arguably the hardest-working room in the house. People come and go at all hours of the day and night, water gets splashed around, the air gets humid enough to grow mold and peel wallpaper right off the walls. No wonder the bathroom is also the most frequently remodeled room in the house.

Time was, all this activity took place in a nondescript, utilitarian room not much bigger than a closet (remember the term *water closet?*). After being fitted with a tub, toilet, and vanity, the roughly 5-ft. by 7-ft. space that evolved out of the post—World War II building boom just didn't offer much room for design creativity.

For several generations of new homeowners, having a hand in the design of their home's bathrooms didn't mean much more than choosing the colors. A major overhaul meant new vinyl on the floor, a new vanity, or maybe new pink or blue fixtures instead of the old white ones.

Today, a stroll through a bath showroom or a quick look at some of the bathrooms featured in this book proves that those days are long gone. Forget great rooms and kitchens; bathrooms are the new frontier in home design. Working couples, traditional, blended, and extended families, the young and old and physically disadvantaged—we all have greater expectations for the places in which we live. We want our bathrooms to be beautiful *and* functional. Easy to clean. A refuge from our busy lives. In response, bathrooms are getting bigger, offering more features, using a wider variety of better materials, and becoming more fun to look at and more pleasant to spend time in.

If you're planning to create a new bathroom or remodel an existing one, you're looking for ideas that will help you transform this room from the merely utilitarian to a personal space that fits your needs. That's where this book comes in. Think of it as a guided tour of some of the most beautiful and creative bathrooms being built today. The tour guides? Some of the best designers and architectural photographers in the business.

Bathrooms today are asked to serve many different functions, from the most mundane to the almost spiritual. My 10-year-old son uses our bathroom as a refuge, a quiet place to read where his younger sister can't bother him. She, in turn, uses it as an entertainment center, a place to apply lipstick and nail polish to her 5-year-old face and fingernails (and different parts of the bathroom itself).

When I'm not picking up after the both of them in there, I'm thinking about ways that it could be improved. What if the lighting were better, more flattering at the vanity, not quite so bright over the toilet and dim in the shower? What if there was better storage for clean towels and more hooks for the wet towels lying on the floor (as well as some device that would automatically pick them up)? How about shelves for the books my son loves to read, more

drawers for my daughter's brightly colored cosmetics? What if there were a built-in step stool, or a lower sink, or a bigger mirror so that she wouldn't have to climb up onto the countertop? What if the tub had a handheld shower as well as the fixed showerhead, making it easier to clean both my daughter and the tub afterward? And while we're at it, why not get rid of that crummy shower curtain?

My musings about bathrooms aren't exactly idle ones; I build them (among other things) when I'm not writing about construction. Not long ago, I contracted with some friends to renovate one of the bathrooms in their house. Although I approached this particular job with some trepidation (working for friends and relatives is always a potential disaster), everybody seemed happy with the finished result. But one of the things that irked me was that I had few visual references for some of the ideas that I was trying to convey to my clients. While we did finally manage to filter out ideas from previous projects, magazines, and manufacturer's product catalogs—all good sources to refer to—I know that this book would have been extremely helpful in the design process.

Like my friends, what you're looking for is ideas; that's why you've picked up this book. What you'll find here are different approaches to bathroom layout, styles, and colors. You'll learn about different finish materials. About different kinds of fixtures. About cabinetry and storage. Even about lighting. Some of these ideas will seem pretty esoteric—how many of us with children will rest easy with a glass sink in the house, for example?—while others may seem pretty mundane. The point is, there are dozens of details that go into making a successful bathroom, and what works in one situation might not be appropriate in another. What you are holding here is a compendium of details, ideas that look good and work well together. Ideas that just might work well in your bathroom.

This isn't a book about wildly impractical, pie-in-the-sky bathrooms for the rich and famous (although there are some of those as well). These are, for the most part, working bathrooms (rather than stylized spaces) designed by professionals for a wide variety of clients and intended to express different ideas about the different elements that go into each bathroom project. Chances are, you'll find some ideas that correspond with your own notions about what is important in this most personal and intimate of spaces. Other ideas you'll reject outright. In either event, you should find plenty of inspiration, as well as practical and essential information, for planning your own bathroom.

Large, small, or somewhere in between, there's a bathroom in here—or some part of it—like the one that you're thinking about. Now is the time to stop dreaming about that new bathroom and start doing something about it.

GREAT BATHROOM DESIGNS

To begin with, throw everything you think you know about bathrooms right out the window. Creating a new bathroom isn't rocket science, but it is more complicated than it used to be back in the days of one-size-fits-all bathroom design. Today's bathrooms are more idiosyncratic, more apt to reflect the personality and lifestyle of their users. There are more choices to be made about fixtures, finishes, cabinetry, and lighting than ever before. Great bathrooms don't just happen; they happen by design.

That process should begin not by shopping for fixtures (though that can be a lot of fun and a great way to get ideas and inspiration) but by defining the space and its intended use. Will it be a small powder room for guests and only occasional use? Will it be a high-traffic family bath, used by both kids and adults? Will it be a master bathroom, used by a working couple jockeying for space during the morning rush hour?

Once you know the room's basic footprint and purpose, it's time to figure out how best to organize everything that you want to go in it. Should the toilet go *here* or *there*? Is there room for both a tub *and* a separate shower, or should you combine them? In a successful bath design, the space shouldn't look or feel cramped, even though it may be small. Of course, there are clearance guidelines that will help you arrange the space; you'll find them in this chapter. And as the basic plan begins to evolve, you'll see how different design principles—the use of color, light, and texture, for example—can affect the way the bathroom looks and feels. Finally, you'll see how bathrooms can be made safer and more user-friendly.

GLASS BLOCK, wood cabinets, carpeting, and tile each introduce a different textural element that contrasts with the hard, smooth surface of the walls and countertop.

CONVENIENT STORAGE is an important part of any bathroom. When there's space, above-counter drawers offer ready access to frequently used items. The nearby walk-in closet is a convenient addition to any bath.

TILE protects against splashes and defines the toilet and tub area. The monochromatic color scheme helps to unify the space.

GRAB BARS play a key role in universal design but are useful for everybody, especially in slippery areas. Accessibility and safety for users of all ages should be important considerations in any bathroom design.

DEFINING THE BATH

1 Functional (note the large walk-in shower) and practical (note the telephone), a master bath can also be a stylish, light-filled refuge. Plants thrive in the moist environment of a bathroom and add a warm, organic touch.

THE TRADITIONAL WAY to describe the bathrooms in a home—full bath (with a tub), ³/₄-bath (with a shower), and ¹/₂-bath (with just a sink and a toilet)—doesn't do justice to the range of baths being designed and built today. It's better to think in terms of function. Family (or general-purpose) baths usually contain both a tub and a shower, often combined into one fixture; master baths, which are typically intended for use primarily by an individual or a couple, often include both a tub and a separate shower. Children's baths are a relatively recent phenomenon, while guest baths and powder rooms usually see only occasional use.

2 A curved glass door offers a dramatic entry to this shower enclosure.

3 Tucking a tub into a gable dormer creates a cozy nook in an otherwise unusable space. Extending the horizontal line of the tile around the room makes this compact bath feel larger.

4 While the bathing area (shown at left) is a natural extension of the adjoining bedroom, the toilet enclosure (top right) has its own door for privacy. Next to the toilet (but not shown) is a separate shower enclosure.

1 Tile wainscot is a durable and easily cleaned surface and adds visual interest to this compact bath with basic floor plan.

2 Guest baths and powder rooms typically see only light use, so the maple countertop in this antique post-and-beam Cape is less likely to be damaged by water than in a family bath.

3 Adding furniture to the bathroom—in this case, a freestanding bureau and open shelving—softens the austerity of tile, porcelain, and vitreous china in this hardworking family bath. Although this is a relatively small room, the large skylight makes it feel more spacious.

4 Annexing a former closet made more room for the luxurious shower and bathing area. A frameless tempered-glass shower enclosure separates the wet area from the rest of this long, narrow bathroom but still leaves the room with an open feeling.

5 White fixtures, easily maintained finishes (such as the one-piece acrylic tub and tile floor), and brightly colored accents and accessories keep this children's bathroom light, clean, and fun.

6 A whimsical wall mural and a fabric valance below the countertop add a fairy-tale touch to this children's bath.

FAMILY/GENERAL-PURPOSE BATHS

1 Placing the sink diagonally in the corner, extending the countertop over the top of the toilet, and adding a large mirror transforms the basic footprint of this 5-ft. by 9-ft. family bath into an intriguing space (floor plan below).

2 This corner shower is built in a confined space, but half-height walls, a small window to the outside, and a simple transparent shower curtain keep it from feeling claustrophobic. The peeled logs add a fun and funky touch.

3 A neo-angle corner shower is a space-saving alternative to the more traditional combination tub/shower that would normally occupy the space. Along with the dramatic skylight well it offers a less-confined feeling to the bathroom.

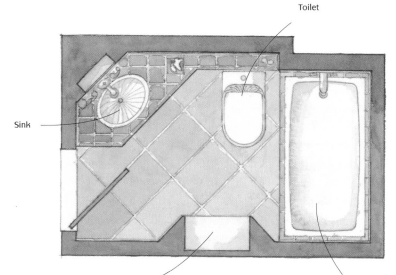

Toilet

Sink

12-in.-deep cabinet recessed into stud bay

Tub/shower

4 Though this isn't a large bathroom, it feels elegant and spacious. Large mirrors in the vanity area help, as do the glass corner shower enclosure and light-colored finish materials.

5 Black and white adds a classic touch to any bathroom. The tile floor, wainscot, and custom shower are not only elegant but also durable, sanitary, and easy to clean.

WHAT WILL IT COST?

Let's not beat around the bush: Bathroom construction and re-modeling can be expensive propositions. After all, bathrooms are complicated spaces laced with extensive plumbing, electrical, heating, and ventilation systems and lots of expensive finish materials. Some new bathing fixtures (tub, shower, toilet, and sink) can cost as much as a small car. So what can you get for your money?

• $1,000 and under: Plan on cosmetic surgery only: new paint and perhaps a new toilet or sink. In this price range, you might also be able to replace a shower door or install new flooring.

• $1,000 to $2,500: Projects in this price range will generally be limited to the existing layout, so don't plan on moving walls or fixtures. You might replace the toilet and sink, for example, and still have money left over for new cabinets, flooring, and paint. Or you might upgrade the tub, either with a new acrylic unit or a new tile surround on an existing tub.

• $2,500 to $7,500: You can make some major changes in this price range, including a new suite of fixtures and new (but moderately priced) finish materials—as long as you don't change fixture locations or try to move walls. Juggling wish lists with the hard realities of cost is a big part of mid-range bathroom projects.

• $7,500 to $12,000: Gutting an existing bathroom, changing fixture locations, and installing new fixtures can easily put you in this price range. You should also be able to replace an old window or add a skylight.

• $12,000 to $20,000: If you're making major architectural changes, like adding a bump-out or converting porch or closet space, then plan on beginning in this price range. Premium materials or fixtures can also quickly bump up the price of a basic remodel into this range.

• $20,000 and up: Start thinking saunas and steamshowers, marble and granite. The sky's the limit!

MASTER-BATH SUITES

1 This master bath is connected to the adjoining bedroom by a pair of French doors. The high ceiling, skylight, and transom window combine to establish a sense of openness and drama.

2 It isn't unusual for a master-bath suite to feature a separate toilet compartment. This convenience enables a couple to comfortably use the room at the same time while maintaining a degree of privacy for each.

3 With a warm wood finish and cabinet-grade detailing, the connection between this bath and adjoining bedroom is clear.

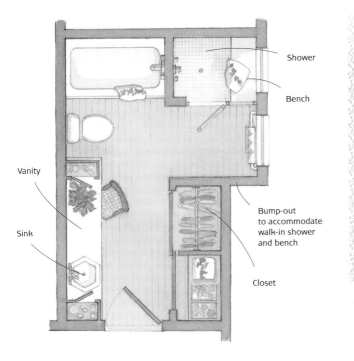

Vanity

Sink

Shower

Bench

Bump-out
to accommodate
walk-in shower
and bench

Closet

4 Beaded wainscoting, frame and raised-panel cabinetry, a wood floor, and a delicate ivy-pattern wallpaper endow this bath with a sense of elegant comfort. The vanity soffit continues over the tub, helping to define the area and to make it feel more intimate (photo at lower left); the soffit also houses recessed lighting fixtures. An exterior wall was bumped out 2 ft. to make room for the tiled shower, which has a solid-surface bench (floor plan at left).

CREATING SPACE

Bathrooms are typically assigned less space than any other room in the house, so one of the biggest design challenges is finding room for everything. Toilets, tubs, showers, and sinks each require a minimum amount of space above and beyond their actual physical dimensions in order to be used properly (see p. 23 for clearance guidelines). While it may be tempting to try to bend those guidelines to squeeze a desired fixture into a smaller-than-recommended space, this is usually a mistake.

When space becomes an issue (as it usually does), there are a few options available. Smaller fixtures can be substituted for larger ones—a shower instead of a tub, for example—while some fixtures can be omitted altogether. Instead of a separate bidet, why not consider a seat-mounted personal hygiene system. And is an extra sink really necessary?

A second option is to annex space from an adjoining area. Often, a closet or hallway that shares a wall with a bathroom can be converted into extra space without too much expense. And adjoining bedrooms can usually spare a few extra square feet to add valuable space to the bath.

A third option is to create space, either by converting a formerly unused area—an attic above a garage, for example—or by building an addition. While a full-sized addition usually requires a foundation (and therefore considerable expense), exterior walls can often be "bumped out" as much as 2 ft. without a foundation—a cost-effective alternative to a larger room addition. In the bathroom featured on this page, a 2-ft.-wide by 7-ft.-long bump-out added 14 sq. ft. of floor area, enough to add a shower area to the existing bathroom.

2 Fitted like a small kitchen, this master bath features plenty of storage and countertop space. Translucent glass block helps keep the shower enclosure from being a dominating presence in the room.

1 Though there isn't room for a separate toilet compartment, a partition wall separates the side-by-side sinks from the toilet in this master bath. Note the mirror-mounted wall sconces.

3 Separated by a corner tub that offers a dramatic cityscape of downtown Tacoma, Wash., these twin vanities reduce the stress level when a couple shares a master bath. Basket-weave accent tiles on the tub surround and a sponged and ragged paint finish on the walls pick up the texture introduced by the nylon wall-to-wall carpeting and Oriental wool rug.

4 Cheerful yellow walls, a vaulted ceiling, a generously sized plate-glass mirror, and a dramatic pentagonal window over the bathing area fill this master bath with light.

5 A ³/₄-in.-thick laminated crackled-glass countertop cantilevers out from the limestone-tiled wall to help support a pair of glass sinks in this spacious master bath. The burgundy finish on the cherry cabinetry stands out against the lighter tones of the rest of the room.

CHILDREN'S BATHS

1 With plenty of room for play, this spacious shower also has practical features, like multiple shower heads, controls mounted near the door, and grab bars for safety. These make the shower useful for washing both kids and the occasional pet.

2 Playful painted animal murals make this bath appealing to kids of all ages.

3 This boat has a soft-sided tub inside to cushion against falls, while its higher 18-in.-high *gunwales* prevent toddlers from falling in. Raising the tub a few inches makes it easier on attending adults to clean little bodies.

4 Grab bars and towel hooks in bright colors are fun and help cut down on bathroom clutter.

5 Kids do a lot of splashing about, so choose finish materials that are water-resistant and easily cleaned, like tile.

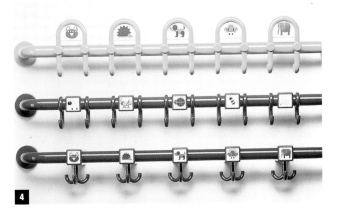

BATHROOM SAFETY

Here's a sobering fact: 25% of home accidents occur in the bathroom, making it one of the most dangerous areas in the home. The most frequent type of accident? Slipping or falling while getting in or out of the tub. Here are a few things you can do to reduce the level of risk in a bathroom:

• Be sure that grab bars are properly installed in appropriate locations.

• Use slip-resistant materials and surfaces in wet areas.

• Turn the home's water temperature down to 120°F. Water heaters are often set to temperatures as high as 150°F, which can cause an instant third-degree burn for a child.

• Be sure tub and shower valves are temperature- or pressure-regulating, so that sudden changes in water temperature don't occur.

• Keep medicines and cleaning products out of the bathroom. Cabinets that do contain medicines should be high out of the reach of children and lockable.

• Be sure that there is a functional ground fault circuit interrupter (GFCI) protecting bathroom electrical circuitry.

• On bathroom doors, use only privacy locks that can be quickly and easily opened in the case of an emergency.

• Don't leave water standing unattended in the tub or sink when there are small children around. Remember that toilets also present a drowning hazard to toddlers; toilet locks are available to reduce the risk.

GUEST BATHS/POWDER ROOMS

1 Inspired by an ornate carved box, this jewel-like powder room features a painted faux-tortoise-shell curved-front vanity. The vanity is inlaid with ivory and topped with a St. Laurent marble countertop. Mirrors on the ceiling and back wall reflect an antique gilt 18th-century French carved mirror.

2 The painted plywood cutout butler welcomes guests and adds a fun sense of formality to this guest bath. Lavish greenery extending down from the wallpaper is actually epoxy paint used to repair old, cracked wall tiles.

A MATTER OF PRIVACY

Privacy is, inexplicably, one factor often overlooked in bathroom design. Large, open spaces look great, but most people prefer some privacy with their drama. Fortunately, it isn't difficult to offer degrees of separation between the public and private spaces that exist in a bathroom.

Doorway placement for single-user baths (such as guest baths and powder rooms) should be planned so that there's a transition area between the private space of a bath and a very public space, such as a kitchen or great room. When possible, these doorways should open into a hallway or smaller room (such as a den or guest bedroom). Also, most designers try to place the toilet out of the line of sight of an open door, usually by situating the fixture behind the door when it is open, or in a separate nook.

Large bathrooms also benefit from transition areas and compartmentalization. If there's room, a separate space with its own door for a toilet is a good idea, making the bathroom comfortably usable by more than one person. Even if there isn't room for a separate enclosure, a nook can often be planned that provides at least a semi-private space for the toilet.

And while tubs may look dramatic in the center of a room, most people aren't totally comfortable being naked up on a stage. It's better to situate a tub in an alcove or corner. Dropping the ceiling near the tub is another way to help psychologically enclose the space and create a greater sense of intimacy.

3 The granite countertop and stainless-steel sink have a commercial feel, but this small room is warmed by the cherry-veneer plywood walls. Note the absence of a backsplash, probably not a necessity in a guest bath that receives only occasional use.

4 Mirrors fronted by wrought-iron gates flank a pecan-wood vanity in this elegantly appointed powder room.

5 The upholstered chair and end table offer a comfortable and informal sitting area in this guest bath.

BATHROOM PLANNING

THE EFFICIENT USE OF SPACE and the proper use of materials are extremely important in the bathroom. For example, squeezing a toilet into a space that is a few inches too small will result in a fixture that may be uncomfortable (or impossible) for some people to use. Choosing the wrong material—a tile that is too slippery for flooring, for example—can make the space unsafe.

All of these situations can be forestalled by some planning. Fortunately, there aren't any deep dark secrets to the process. Widely accepted clearance guidelines (you'll find some on the facing page) will help you place fixtures, and accessibility and safety guidelines will help to ensure that the room is user-friendly and safe for all. Now is also the time to think about how to enhance the appearance of the space with elements of design.

1 Adding seating and grab bars in the tub and shower areas dramatically enhances accessibility for those with physical disabilities and safety for everyone.

2 A high ceiling, extensive use of white tile, and large, dramatically arched windows make this bathroom light and airy. Colorful tile accents and curves soften the geometry and ensure that the space doesn't feel stark or clinical.

RECOMMENDED CLEARANCES FOR FIXTURES The clearances shown are intended to provide adequate room for access and maneuvering for people with (or without) disabilities.

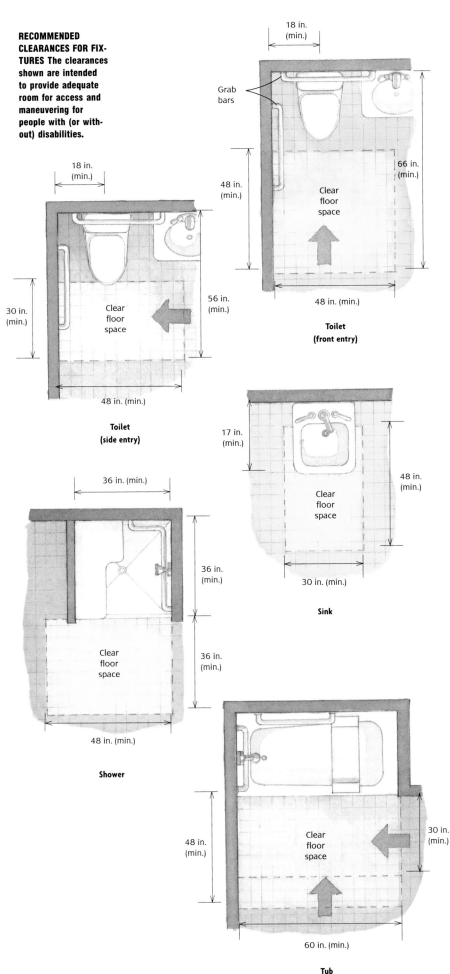

18 in. (min.)

30 in. (min.)

Clear floor space

48 in. (min.)

Toilet (side entry)

18 in. (min.)

Grab bars

66 in. (min.)

48 in. (min.)

Clear floor space

56 in. (min.)

48 in. (min.)

Toilet (front entry)

17 in. (min.)

Clear floor space

48 in. (min.)

30 in. (min.)

Sink

36 in. (min.)

36 in. (min.)

36 in. (min.)

Clear floor space

48 in. (min.)

Shower

48 in. (min.)

Clear floor space

30 in. (min.)

60 in. (min.)

Tub (front or side entry)

VISUAL SPACE

The bathroom is typically a small room, filled with bulky fixtures that take up a lot of visual space. Designers recognize that the actual physical size of a room (its *shape*) can be enhanced by the skillful use of placement, texture, pattern, and color, making its apparent size (its *form*) feel either larger or smaller. Here are a few simple ways to make a small space feel larger:

• Keep walls and floors a light color. By reducing or eliminating contrast (for example, by avoiding bright or dark-colored fixtures next to white walls) the perception of space is enhanced.

• Use patterns made up of small elements (small tiles, for example), which tend to give the impression of being farther away.

• Keep vertical lines to a minimum—they tend to add height to a room and make the floor space seem smaller. Emphasize horizontal lines (vanity tops, shelving, and cabinets), which tend to visually expand the space. Aligning the tops of mirrors, doors and windows, and tub or shower enclosures establishes a dominant horizontal direction.

• Use mirrors to help visually expand the space and transform structural barriers into reflective surfaces. Floor-to-ceiling mirrors increase the apparent room height, while mirrors placed along one or two long walls will widen a narrow room.

• Repeating design elements—color, pattern, texture, size—makes a space feel more unified, and therefore larger.

3 A single accent color—in this case blue—adds visual interest to a light-colored room. The shower area has a low curb, a folding seat, and grab bars for safer and more accessible use.

2 Extending the countertop over the top of the toilet adds both practical storage space and a strong horizontal element to balance the high ceiling. The large mirror and the row of lighting above it visually expand the room.

1 Virtually unchanged since its addition to a Federal-style New England brick house in the 1920s, this light-filled, old-fashioned bath maintains its sunny disposition. Note how the texture and orange/yellow tones in the wood floor help warm the room.

CHOOSING COLORS AND TEXTURES

The intimate red glow of a sunset, the cozy feeling of flannel sheets, smooth as silk, cool blue.... More than just words, colors and textures suggest ideas that have an emotional impact. Designers have long realized that color and texture can be incorporated into interior design to evoke certain moods. Here are a few guidelines to help you sort out what colors and textures can do for your bathroom.

When we think of *texture,* we think of touching something—a rough piece of bark, a smooth stone, a soft cotton towel. But texture also involves a visual response and memory, and designers use this effect in several different ways. For example, texture can be used to suggest different characteristics, such as masculinity (hard surfaces) or femininity (soft surfaces), simplicity (irregular and dull finishes) or refinement (even or shiny surfaces). Just think of the feminine quality that the use of fabric brings to a room.

Texture can also be used to provide contrast and variety to an otherwise uniform surface. For example, the rough, sandy surface of grout contrasts with the hard, smooth, and reflective surface of tile in a way that suggests an overall composition, rather than a single surface. In another less subtle example, a simple painted drywall surface can be transformed by decoratively applied paint (such as sponging or rag rolling) or a wall-covering.

Color is often the most memorable feature of an interior design. Our psychological reactions to it are linked to primitive associations with nature. Red, like fire, can suggest danger and is exciting.

Blue, like ice, is mysterious and suggests calm. Yellow, like sunshine, is cheerful; green is associated with plants and grass and is peaceful and mellow. Warm brown tones suggest the earth.

Colors on the red side of the spectrum are generally thought to be warm, while colors on the blue side of the spectrum are thought to be cool. Greens are typically neutral, but there are warm greens (which contain red) and cool greens (which contain more blue than yellow). Blues can be warmed with the addition of red, just as the temperature of other colors can be modified.

Few spaces are monochromatic, so using color effectively requires an understanding of how different colors interact with one another. The color wheel, which breaks down light into 12 basic colors, is often used to establish relationships between them. For example, the three primary colors—red, yellow, and blue—are the most intense and are spaced equidistantly around the color wheel. Arranged in between are the secondary and tertiary colors. A complementary color scheme would feature colors opposite each other on the color wheel, while an analogous scheme would feature adjacent colors. White, black, and gray, are considered non-colors, but they are used extensively in bathroom design.

Colors are seen truly only in natural daylight. So artificial lighting has an effect on color as well, both by having its own color temperature and by its intensity, since dim light tends to neutralize color. (For more on lighting, see pp. 138-147.)

3 White tile provides a practical, water-resistant finish for tubs, but it can have a clinical feel. Here, the rough texture and orange/yellow tone of the pine-paneled walls and window trim add warmth and simplicity to the bathroom.

5 Grays and shades of white complement the spare simplicity of this design. The suite of wall-hung, accessibility-designed fixtures offer plenty of clearance underneath and are easy to clean.

4 Repeating patterns and colors unify this design, while the darker contrasting tiles provide interest. The strong horizontal line introduced by the tile chair rail balances the high ceiling and skylight, which otherwise might make the room feel too tall.

ELEMENTS OF GOOD DESIGN

2 Even though darker surfaces tend to compress a space, the small tiles in this bathroom balance that effect and offer contrast to the white walls. Unusual angles add interest, while the high window lets in light without compromising privacy.

1 Cool colors—like the purple-blue of this bathroom tile—evoke a serene and introspective feeling.

3 Natural colors and materials create a sense of warmth, while the wall-hung vanity, skylights, and windows enhance the open character of the bath. Circular mirrors are adjustable and contrast with the rectangular shapes that dominate the room.

4 Gray slate on the floor and in the shower area provides a neutral, rough-textured contrast to the wood finishes and warm yellow wall surfaces. Note the light fixture unobtrusively located in the skylight well, which provides a diffuse source of general overhead natural and artificial lighting around the clock.

1 While the blue floral cushions and white raised-panel cabinetry introduce a cool and rather formal element to this bathroom suite, the fabric's texture and the informality of a sitting area make this bath feel warmer and more inviting.

2 Steps leading up to a bath look elegant but increase the risk of slips and falls. The narrower second step and extended shelves on either side offer hand support when entering and exiting this whirlpool, though grab bars in the tub and shower area would be easier to grasp.

3 A serene oasis for two busy physicians, this basement bathroom's sage-green walls temper the more antiseptic marble tile found on the radiantly heated floor, lower walls, and soaking tub platform. The window high in the upper left-hand corner brings in light, while an automatic humidistat-controlled ventilation fan takes care of unwanted humidity.

5 Large windows and cheerful yellow walls fill the room with daylight and balance the darker natural wood finish on the ceiling, Douglas fir countertop, floor, and door. The door leads to a private toilet compartment.

4 Dark colors can make small spaces seem even smaller, but the high ceiling balances the warm tones of this intimate bath, making it feel inviting rather than claustrophobic.

ORGANIZING THE SPACE

1 A tiny (7-ft. by 7-ft.) guest bathroom is carved out of the corner of a guest bedroom located above a garage. Moving the toilet out from the knee wall provides storage behind it and creates a little more headroom, while the sliding pocket door doesn't intrude on the limited floor space.

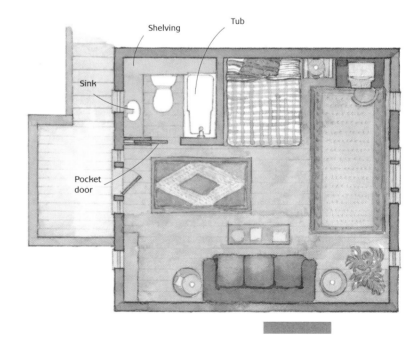

Shelving

Tub

Sink

Pocket door

3 A shower wall helps to create a semi-private nook for the toilet. Notice the glass panel, which allows light from the exterior window to enter the shower yet still offers privacy.

2 Open glass shelving tucked into an unused corner behind the door utilizes space that is normally wasted and provides easy access to often-used items like towels and toiletries.

4 Contained in its own enclosure, the toilet offers privacy and helps to separate the shower area from the sink, a useful feature when a bath is used by a couple.

ACCESSIBILITY & SAFETY

1 Bright colors and high-quality finishes keep this universally accessible bathroom from looking institutional. The console-style sink offers both open floor space beneath the fixture and protection from contact with hot water pipes. A mirror extends down to backsplash level (top photo at right). The shower area features a curbless design for easy wheelchair access and a shower curtain that pulls almost completely out of the way (bottom photo at right).

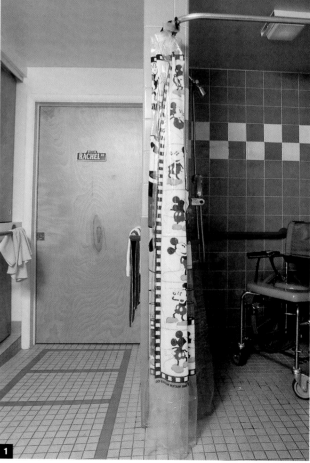

Curbless shower

Continuous countertop doubles as grab bar.

Offset drain

Continuous grab bar

Grab bar

Ramp to different level

Grab bars

Window

Pocket door

Storage

A COMPACT ACCESSIBLE BATHROOM
Bathrooms intended for use by wheelchair users need to be fitted with grab bars and have enough room for entry and exit.

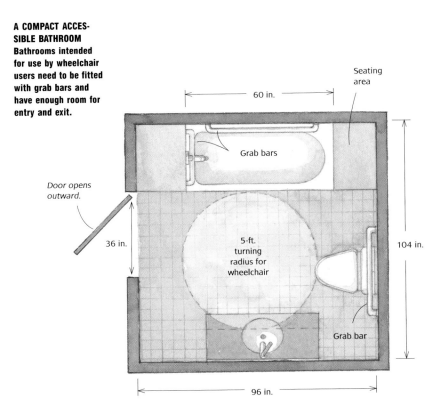

Seating area

60 in.

Grab bars

Door opens outward.

36 in.

5-ft. turning radius for wheelchair

104 in.

Grab bar

96 in.

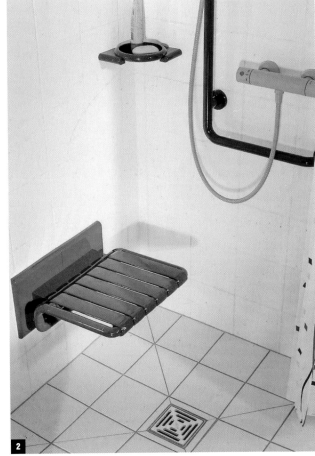

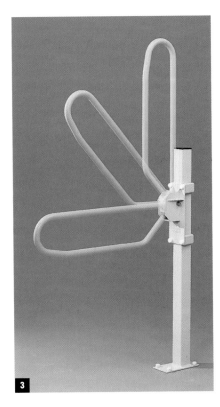

2

2 This shower seat folds out of the way when not in use, allowing the shower to be used in either a standing or seated position. Note the color-coordinated L-shaped grab bar mounted nearby.

3 Grab bars are available in a number of styles and colors and offer safe support to all ages and abilities. This floor-mounted model can be installed near a toilet and swings out of the way when not in use.

3

UNIVERSAL ACCESSIBILITY

Accessibility should be a design consideration in every bathroom. Here's why: As families and individuals age, their needs change. Small children become adults; adults become the elderly. Unfortunately, the built environment is geared primarily toward adults in perfect health, which accounts for less than a quarter of the population. For the remaining 75%, physical limitations sometimes make it difficult, if not impossible, to use the facilities that many of us take for granted.

While people can adapt to some extent to their environment, a better and safer approach is to adapt the environment to meet the changing needs of those using it. Accessibility doesn't necessarily require extensive modifications or expensive fixtures or accessories. In fact, an accessible bathroom need not even look accessi-

ble. Here's a list of modifications to typical bathroom designs that will result in more accessible facilities for a wider range of abilities:

• Install grab bars. Make sure that structural backing is included before walls are finished in potential grab-bar locations (tub/shower area, toilet area, and near the sink).

• Consider using lever handles for doors and fixtures rather than round knobs, which can be difficult to grasp.

• Be sure that minimum fixture clearance guidelines are followed (see p. 23).

• Avoid narrow doorways and passageways, as well as thresholds at doorways or changes in floor-surface elevations.

• Locate tub and shower controls so they can be operated either from within or outside the unit. Also, be sure that the controls are not so

high that they would be unusable for a person in a seated position.

• Locate switches, outlets, and other controls so they can be easily accessed by someone in a seated position. This means placing switches slightly lower than normal and outlets slightly higher than normal.

• Provide seating in both the tub and shower areas.

• Consider using a sink design that offers knee space below the sink.

• Provide a handheld shower in addition to a fixed showerhead.

• Use tilting mirrors, full-height mirrors, or make sure that mirrors extend all the way down to sink level.

• Provide easily accessible storage (both drawers and cabinetry) between 15 in. and 48 in. off the floor.

FINISHING THE BATH IN STYLE

Style is as much a feeling as it is a look. Think of the hygienic, almost clinical feel of gleaming white fixtures and spotless tile floors and walls. Or the country charm of billowy cotton curtains and varnished pine. The sleek sophistication of polished surfaces like marble and granite. Choosing a style and deciding on finish materials for the bathroom go hand in hand.

How do you settle on a specific style? Picture the places you feel most comfortable in, the cultures you admire, the eras that you find most interesting. You'll find plenty of examples of different bathroom styles in this chapter to help refine your own conclusions. You'll also find that you can mix and match styles—for example, a clawfoot tub is just as comfortable in a contemporary bath as it is in a traditional setting.

You can mix and match finish materials as well. Tile is still popular and versatile, an all-around choice that can be both beautiful and budget-friendly. But there are other options. How about marble or granite? Although these stones are expensive, most bathrooms are relatively small; a little material will go a long way. Or why not wood? Sure, it's more susceptible to moisture damage than some other finishes, but it's a naturally warm material that can transform a bath. Metals, glass, laminates, solid-surface materials, even concrete, have their place in the bath. How do you choose? Take a tour through the baths on the following pages and see how others have used the palette of natural and synthetic finish materials to create bathrooms of style and substance.

GLASS shower enclosures have a spare, contemporary look and let in plenty of light, making them a good choice in a small bathroom. The clear frameless door panels slide rather than swing, so they don't drip water onto the floor when they're open.

GRANITE is a
durable and stain-
resistant surface
that's perfect for a
wet environment.
Here, warm, earth-
toned wall tiles
complement the
cherry countertop.
The white granite
floor tiles have a
slip-resistant satin
surface.

STAINLESS STEEL
has a modern
industrial quality
that matches the
other finishes in
this bathroom.
The shiny surface
of the sink pro-
vides a visual
focus to the bath
and balances the
polished chrome of
the plumbing and
shower fixtures.

CHERRY adds a
warm and richly
textured counter-
point to the cool
materials that pre-
dominate in this
bathroom. The
sink's open design
and the exposed
plumbing are in
keeping with the
bathroom's con-
temporary style.

TAKING A LOOK AT STYLE

1 A graceful French chandelier, billowing balloon valances, and fabrics and wallcoverings that capture the colors of the ocean and gardens just outside the windows add an element of Victorian romance to what was once a child's bedroom. The restored wood floor has both a warm color and an elegant look.

2 Earth tones, organic materials, and terra-cotta tile characterize the Southwestern style. A frameless glass shower enclosure is an unabashed concession to the demands of modern life, while the more traditional clawfoot tub suggests a slower-paced time.

WHEN WE THINK OF STYLE, we might think of a specific historical period and of the architectural features that characterize it. In this chapter, for example, we'll take a look at both contemporary and period bathrooms, examining the characteristics that distinguish one bath as modern, another as Craftsman-style, and a third as perhaps Shaker-style.

But style is more than just an architectural reference to a particular place and time. After all, before 1920, most houses didn't even have bathrooms, so the idea of a period bathroom really depends more on stylistic interpretations that re-create the mood or ambience of these earlier spaces, rather than literal architectural reproduction.

3 Part fantasy, partly inspired by Moroccan architecture, the vaulted ceiling of this bathroom has the draped look and feel of a sheik's tent, but it is actually constructed of traditional plaster with a painted finish. The floor is finished with a handmade smoked terra-cotta tile, while an antique Moroccan lamp hangs from the ceiling.

4 Forged black-iron hardware stands out against the washed white pine vanity and lends a casual Scandinavian country influence to this bath. The countertop is a light marble; the flooring is southern yellow pine, also with a washed finish.

5 Shoji screens separate the sauna, toilet, and laundry areas from the rest of this Japanese-style bathhouse. Large slate tiles are good conductors for the radiant heating beneath the floor and have a rich, rough texture that helps connect this space to the outdoors.

1 A glass-block wall separates the marble-tiled bathing area from the shower enclosure behind it in this carpeted contemporary bath. Twin his-and-hers vanities flank the opening from the master bedroom, while a door to the right opens onto a deck.

2 Adjustable mirrors add a touch of style and class to morning and evening grooming rituals.

3 Simple touches—beaded paneling, a salvaged pedestal sink, and an antique mirror—give this bath in a rehabilitated 150-year-old Vermont barn the look needed to meet historic preservation approval.

4 Design details like the arched frames over the large window and mirror go a long way toward defining a bathroom's style. Hardworking materials like the ceramic-tile backsplash and solid-surface countertop have a place in both contemporary and traditional baths.

5 Finely detailed alderwood cabinetry and a vaulted Douglas fir ceiling lend a romantic tone to this southern California bath built in the Spanish-colonial tradition.

1 A refuge from the rest of the house, this attic bath is filled with objects from the owner's travels. Low-maintenance silk greenery and vintage fabrics from the 1930s soften the crisp feel of the glossy white paneling.

2 The cabinet detailing, corner-mounted sink, and strong horizontal element introduced by the wallpaper border transform a simple space into an interesting one. The stegosaurus is optional.

3 This contemporary and compact bath celebrates the bold geometry and Art Deco flavor of contrasting black-and-white tile.

WHETHER YOUR TASTES lean toward contemporary or traditional styles, good bathroom design should reflect your own individuality and imagination and express your own tastes and interests. More than a particular look, the bathroom will then end up reflecting a certain quality—such as formal or romantic—that makes the room an interesting and desirable place to be. Go ahead and pay attention to styles and traditions, but don't be afraid to experiment by mixing and matching stylistic elements and old and new materials as well. Formal or informal, traditional or eclectic, the best style is ultimately your own style.

4 Hand-glazed terra-cotta tiles in a palette of colors enrich this artist's studio bath.

5 Like the early-20th-century Arts and Crafts movement that inspired it, this bath celebrates natural materials, rich organic colors, and details of workmanship that show the hand of the artisan.

PERIOD BATHS

1 Tile, enameled cast iron, and chrome have a traditional feel that is at home in almost any bath. Accessories—like the mirrors and soap rack—help personalize the space.

2 Accents like the folding screen above the cast-iron tub and the gilded mirror add a serene Oriental air to this elegant renovated bath. A raised-panel tub surround topped with Janina marble tile was built around the original freestanding clawfoot tub to hide considerable wall damage and disrepair in the original bath.

3 In this French Cottage–style bathroom, an unusual alderwood vanity with turned legs helps to widen the appearance of the narrow bathroom (floor plan below). The marble countertop has a small, round undermount hammered-pewter sink with matching faucet. The floor tile is limestone.

4 Painted white wainscot, a classic and practical treatment for any bathroom, contrasts with the dark patterned wallpaper on the walls and ceiling. Crown molding and corner blocks on the window trim lend a Victorian air to this otherwise simple bath.

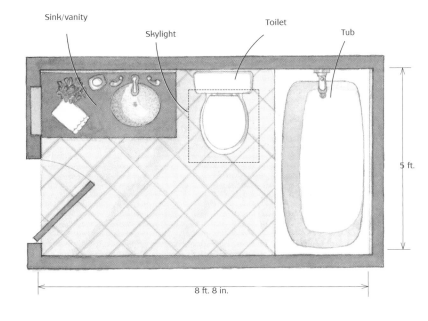

Sink/vanity

Skylight

Toilet

Tub

5 ft.

8 ft. 8 in.

1 A painted blue sky, *trompe l'oeil* columns, and a faux-marble finish on the lower walls suggest a Roman bath. Gauze-like sheers diffuse the light reflecting off the nearby Atlantic Ocean and conceal the view of a too-close roof.

3 Set on a Carrera marble countertop, this polished-nickel lever-handled faucet has an antique look. The mirror above is made of molded glass with an *eglomise* (or reverse-painted) finish.

2 Craftsman-style meets Scandinavia: Continuous trim links the medicine cabinet and window, while the whites, pastels, and simple stencil motif help to unify the design.

4 The gracefully curved sink and a distinctive geometric pattern in the black-and-white floor tile contribute to the Art Deco look of this bathroom (left), while the unusual running-bond pattern of the wall tile adds an unusual twist. The 1920s-style bathroom has been updated with the addition of a handheld shower in the tub area and a separate shower area (above).

1 Custom-fabricated sliding-glass doors connect this contemporary bathroom to the relatively mild California coastal environment, giving the 45-sq.-ft. room a light and airy feel (floor plan facing page). Removable western red-cedar duckboards cover the tiled shower floor.

Sliding-glass door
to outside

Removable
red-cedar
duckboards

Double
shower
heads

Frameless
glass door
and
enclosure

Toilet

Sink

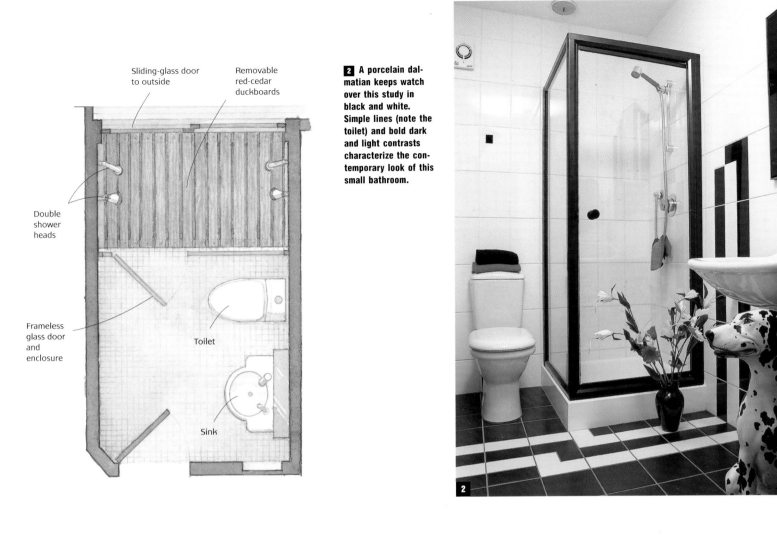

2 A porcelain dalmatian keeps watch over this study in black and white. Simple lines (note the toilet) and bold dark and light contrasts characterize the contemporary look of this small bathroom.

3 Colorful accents highlight this bath's neutral tones and no-nonsense finishes. White faucets hide toothpaste and soap scum and are easy to clean, as is the contrasting Barre gray-granite countertop.

1 Dark, acid-washed copper panels in the frame-and-panel doors contrast with the light maple vanity cabinetry. The panels mirror the color and texture of the slate tile flooring and the above-counter copper sink bowl.

2 While the detailing is traditional, the translucent frameless glass shower enclosure gives this bath a contemporary feel. Tumbled-marble floor tiles have a nonslip texture that makes them appropriate for bathrooms; the countertop is a lighter-colored slab of French vanilla marble.

3 Looking as though it might be at home on the space station Mir, this red molded Italian vanity brightly contrasts with the more subdued—but still contemporary— wall tile.

4 This casually contemporary Napa Valley bathroom has hints of the Mediterranean, including plaster walls, a limestone countertop, rift oak cabinetry, and glazed pavers around the tub.

5 Contemporary baths are often characterized by bold uses of materials, color, and light. In such a setting, traditional elements like this pedestal sink have a comforting presence.

NATURAL FINISH MATERIALS

1 Green cleft-slate tile on the tub surround has a rough-textured surface that contrasts nicely with the smooth finish of the cast-iron whirlpool, adding an organic touch to this rather industrial-looking space. The window glass wraps around the corners and surrounds the space with a 180° view of the San Fernando Valley and distant San Gabriel Mountains.

2 Small square white tile offers a timeless bathroom surface that is bright and easy to clean and never goes out of style. Here, the tile wraps around the window opening, minimizing the chance of water damage to the window.

3 Large spaces generally look better with large tile, but the small black tiles used on this floor and tub area offer dramatic balance to the angular columns, glass-block window wall, and skylit ceiling that enclose the space.

CERAMIC TILE, composed of clay, ground shale or gypsum, and other ingredients from the earth, has a 6,000-year history. It's not likely to go out of style any time soon. Stones such as marble, granite, and slate can also be cut into ceramic-like tiles, though they are also available as larger slabs. Uniformly cut (called gauged) stone is usually polished, while cleft stone has an irregular (and therefore, harder to keep clean) surface.

Wood has a warm, rich color and texture that can offset some of the colder and harder materials, like metal and glass, that are often used in the bathroom. Decay-resistant woods, such as cedar, redwood, and teak, are more suitable for wet areas, but most species can be used in non-critical areas—for cabinets or wall finishes, for example—if properly protected with the right finish.

4 The geometry of the ceramic tile and glass-block shower wall is softened by the graceful curves and texture of the wood trim and treads. Hand-painted ceramic tile completes the composition.

5 An intimate bathing alcove framed with columns and softened by curves introduces a feminine element to the harder surfaces of glass block and highly polished marble on the floor and walls of this elegant master bath.

TILE & STONE

1 Tile is often chosen for its color alone, but it also offers a rich palette of pattern and texture to the resourceful designer.

2 White marble is softer and stains more easily than the contrasting green marble in this bathroom, though scratches are more noticeable in the darker colors.

3 Rough-textured slate tile is a good choice for this floor and tub deck because it provides good traction even when wet. It has an unusual red-brown color that compliments the earth tones found in the other finishes in this bathroom.

4 Slate—a smooth, sedimentary stone composed mainly of clay—can be polished to a beautiful soft sheen, as seen in this naturally edged slab countertop, but it is more commonly available as a rough-textured tile.

5 Cutting a ragged edge with tile nippers creates a fractured edge that helps relieve the rigidly geometric look of ceramic tile. The rough tile edge was finished in place with two coats of appliance touch-up paint.

CHOOSING TILE

Ceramic tile's variety, versatility, and durability make it a popular bathroom finish material. But how do you decide whether to choose a generic 4-in. by 4-in. white tile that costs $1.00/sq. ft. or an almost identical-looking designer tile that needs to be special-ordered at $7.00/sq. ft.? Which tiles are best for floors? Do you need a special tile for the shower?

Permeability, or the ability to absorb moisture, is one way of comparing tile. Vitreous tile has a dense body and absorbs a negligible amount of moisture. It's better suited for wet or exterior installations than nonvitreous tile, which is softer and more porous. Because nonvitreous tile is fired for a shorter period of time at a lower temperature, it's less expensive to manufacture (and therefore to buy) than vitreous tile. In practice, both vitreous and nonvitreous tiles are used interchangeably in the bathroom, since the tile's glaze protects it against most moisture.

Another way of comparing tile is by the relative hardness of its surface. Tile manufacturers use the Mohs scale, which ranges from 1 (the softest) to 10 (the hardest), to grade their tile. Floor tile needs to be more resistant to scratching than wall tile and should rate at least 6 or 7 on the Mohs scale.

Texture should be another concern when choosing tile. Although the shiny smooth surface of a polished or smoothly glazed material may look great and be easy to clean, it can be slippery when wet. It's better to choose a tile that has a textured or matte glaze for floors and save the shiny tiles for the walls and countertops.

When you go to choose tile, you'll notice that some of it is graded and some of it isn't. Standard-grade tile accounts for about 75% of all tile sold and meets standards set by ANSI (American National Standards Institute). Second-grade tile is cheaper than standard grade and may have slight inconsistencies in either its size or glaze, though it is functionally the equivalent of standard-grade tile. Ungraded tile of varying quality is also available. Some of it is perfectly okay to use (Mexican pavers can fall into this category), while some is of decidedly inferior quality. Decorative tile should be used for just that purpose: It's too fragile for functional use.

The best way to choose tile is to know what the tile will be used for, pick out something you like at a tile store, take some samples home, and put them through a few scratching, rubbing, and scuffing tests.

WOOD

1 Oil-finished clear redwood bevel siding on the walls and redwood trim around the tub offer a subtle contrast to the cedar-lined soaking tub. The tub is constructed of pressure-treated plywood and has a vinyl liner concealed beneath the cedar to keep the water in.

2 Beaded hemlock wainscoting with a simple chair rail and baseboard adds a rustic element to this comfortable bath.

3 A poured-on, self-leveling, clear epoxy finish protects the fir countertop of this dormitory-style bath built for three boys. The beaded tongue-and-groove fir paneling, reminiscent of the Adirondack camps admired by the family, is finished with Danish oil.

WOOD FINISHES

Wood has a natural warmth and texture that make it an appealing bathroom finish. Consisting primarily of fine cellular ducts that once carried water and dissolved minerals from the roots upward, wood that has long been cut and milled into lumber still has the capability of absorbing and releasing moisture. This can be bad news, because wood that is exposed to water will begin to decay. Some woods—teak, cedar, and redwood, for instance—are more decay-resistant than others, making them more suitable for the damp environment of a bathroom. But given proper preparation and protection, most wood species have their place in the bath.

Wood flooring offers a warm contrast to some of the other harder and sometimes cold-feeling materials often found in the bathroom. Most common flooring species—oak, maple, cherry, even pine—can be used successfully, given proper preparation and installation. Wide boards shrink and swell more noticeably than narrower ones, so 2¼-in. strip flooring in one of the relatively stable species is less likely than wider plank flooring to be affected by the humidity swings that are common in the bathroom. Choose a coating-type finish, such as polyurethane, that isn't easily affected by standing water and that can be mopped rather than a penetrating-oil finish that is less resistant to water.

Wood can also be used for countertops. It's easily cut, installed, sanded, and repaired, and it's easy on grooming aids and glassware that get dropped onto it. Maple butcher block is a popular ready-made countertop material that is sold by the running foot in varying widths. Other popular countertop woods include teak and redwood. Cutouts for sinks can present a problem unless the cut edge is properly sealed against moisture. Again, a polyurethane-type coating sealant is the best choice for a finish.

Wood is also a good choice as a wall and ceiling covering, though its use in shower areas where it's constantly exposed to moisture is ill-advised. Besides its natural beauty, wood can help soundproof a room and make it feel warmer. Tongue-and-groove wainscoting topped with a chair rail, either painted or clear-coated with polyurethane, offers a traditional treatment that is durable and easily cleaned.

Paneling on walls and/or ceilings is another option. Vertical V-groove paneling has a rustic look and can be installed diagonally or horizontally. Square-edged paneling has a more subtle and contemporary look because of the absence of prominent shadow lines. Bevel-edge siding in cedar or redwood, more commonly used on exterior walls, can also be used to good effect as a wall treatment.

5 Located in the heart of redwood country, this bathroom's highly figured redwood paneling comes from second- and third-growth timber. Large windows in the gable wall, a cathedral ceiling, and skylights light up the darker surface of the wood and preserve the sense of spaciousness.

4 An unusual 3/4-in.-thick sand-blasted glass countertop with a ceramic sink is suspended between twin French-polished black-cherry-veneer cabinets. A lacquer finish protects the cherry-veneer wall, which curves past a Japanese soaking tub and on into the rest of the bathroom suite.

6 Stained to look like old marquetry, this oak hardwood floor's intricate design extends around the corner into the shower and closet area. The countertop and tub deck are of Miel de Ora marble.

GLASS & METAL

1

1 A trident-wielding Neptune etched into the door glass stands guard at the entry to this seaside bathroom (right), while translucent fish swim peacefully past the exterior casement window (above).

1

3 Large windows located high in the gable wall offer a clear view outside and flood this master bath with light. Interior glass-block walls keep the shower from feeling enclosed.

2 An exterior glass-block wall washes this intimate bathing area in color and light. Available in a wide variety of sizes, shapes, colors, and textures, glass block offers privacy and helps to insulate against noise and heat loss.

4 Supported by a welded aluminum frame, this frosted-glass countertop softens the abstract pattern painted on the medium-density fiberboard (MDF) countertop beneath. Drawer pulls anchor the glass panels to the drawer fronts.

OTHER MATERIALS

1 Concrete-block walls provide a solid foundation for the vaulted glass ceiling soaring over this soaking tub in west Los Angeles.

2 Carpet is warm underfoot and is a good flooring choice for areas in the bath that don't get wet. Note that this bathroom has an easily cleaned and dried slate floor under the tub area.

3 Concrete is a versatile and inexpensive material that can be used in a number of different ways. Here, standard copper plumbing pipes support a cast-concrete countertop.

4 Precast concrete block has a rough but even texture and a neutral gray color that focuses attention on the wood in the rest of this bathroom in the Hollywood hills. The exterior door leads to a private courtyard carved out of the hillside.

SYNTHETIC MATERIALS

1 Plastic laminate is right at home in almost any bathroom environment. Widely available and inexpensive, it's popular as a countertop material because it is available in a broad spectrum of colors, patterns, and textures.

2 Solid-surface materials have the appearance and characteristics of stone, yet countertops like this one can be fabricated almost seamlessly using common woodworking tools. The material is durable and stain-resistant, and repairs can be made simply by sanding the affected area.

3 Corian, a mineral-filled acrylic polymer solid-surface material, caps a glass block shower wall. The inside and outside corner seams are chemically welded; like all solid-surface materials, Corian is unaffected by water splashing out from the shower.

4 Plastic-laminate countertops are available with a number of different edge treatments, including this square-edged wood front to match the cabinets.

SYNTHETIC MATERIALS are typically marketed as more widely available or less-expensive substitutes for natural materials. Plastic laminate, for example, is still by far the most popular countertop material in the world. Solid-surface materials were introduced only a couple of decades ago but have become increasingly popular with designers and homeowners. These materials have many of the properties of stone but are more easily fabricated. While far more expensive than plastic laminate and available in only a limited number of colors, solid-surface materials are easily repaired. Like laminate, they can be used in any area of the bathroom.

SOLID-SURFACE MATERIALS

1 Solid-surface sink bowls in different shapes and sizes are available either to match or contrast with solid-surface countertops. They can be joined seamlessly to form an integral countertop that is smooth and easily cleaned. Note the contrasting inlay on the front edge of this countertop.

2 Solid-surface materials can be shaped and sanded like wood (photo, bottom right), while welded joints are virtually invisible. Edge treatments like the contrasting inlay (top right) and the routed edge with matching door pull (middle right) illustrate two possibilities.

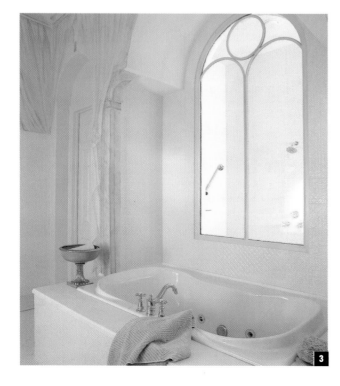

3 Solid-surface materials aren't just for countertops. Here, the tub deck is fabricated from a single sheet of the material.

4 This solid-surface countertop has an undermounted vitreous china sink. A cost-effective 2-ft. bump-out provides enough room for both a shower and a short but deep soaking tub.

ABOUT SOLID-SURFACE MATERIALS

DuPont began the solid-surface revolution some 30-odd years ago when it developed a technique for blending natural minerals with acrylic resin. In addition to DuPont's popular Corian, there are now several other solid-surface materials to choose from, including Formica's Surell and Wilsonart's Gibraltar. While each has different composition, color, and texture, all solid-surface materials share certain qualities and characteristics that make them ideal for a bathroom environment.

Unlike plastic laminates, solid-surface materials can be repaired if they get burned or scratched (simply by sanding and buffing out the defect). They are repairable because the material is nonporous and the color goes all the way

through—making them difficult to stain in the first place. They're unaffected by most chemicals, with the exception of some paint removers and oven cleaners, and are even fairly resistant to heat damage. You probably won't chop onions or set a hot frying pan down on a bathroom countertop, but if you manage to damage it— and it's made of solid-surface material—it can be fixed.

Solid-surface materials are available in $1/4$-in., $1/2$-in., and $3/4$-in. thicknesses of varying lengths and widths. They can be used in a number of bathroom applications besides countertops. For example, their smooth, easily cleaned surface makes them ideal for tub and shower surrounds. Some manufacturers offer thinner $1/8$-in. solid-

surface veneers as a more economical alternative to the full-thickness materials.

Premolded solid-surface sinks are available in a limited number of sizes, shapes, and colors to coordinate with most manufacturer's product lines. Specialty shops can fabricate custom countertops with seamlessly welded integral sinks that match (or contrast with) your chosen countertop material.

A major advantage of solid-surface materials is that they can be readily tooled with standard woodworking machinery. This isn't a job for the faint of heart, though: this stuff is relatively expensive. In addition, some manufacturers won't sell the material to anyone who hasn't completed a fabricator's certification course.

But the ability to cut, shape, turn, rout, sand, and polish solid surface is what makes it unique. Some solid-surface materials can even be molded into custom shapes. And at least one (Corian) is available in liquid form and can be poured into inlay patterns. More and more different ways to use solid-surface materials are being developed every day.

Choosing between the different kinds of solid-surface materials available will require some homework. Don't rely on product literature; get sample kits containing actual small blocks of the material to help you compare the colors and textures that each manufacturer has to offer.

LAMINATES

1 Although typically thought of as a countertop material, plastic laminate is becoming increasingly popular as a flooring option. Some laminates, like Formica's Fired Earth laminate flooring, are approved for use in the bathroom.

When Daniel O'Conor invented plastic laminate as an artificial substitute for the mineral mica back in 1913, his employer, Westinghouse, took little notice. So he and a friend formed a new company to produce the new material and began to think of new applications for it. They called their new product and their new company Formica. In 1927 the first sheets of high-pressure decorative plastic laminate (or HPDL, the technical term for the product) began to appear. It became a popular building material in the postwar building boom of the 1940s and 1950s. Now, it's by far the most popular countertop material around the world.

Plastic laminate is made of several layers of kraft paper, a layer of decorative paper (which provides the color and pattern), and a top protective layer of melamine. This sandwich is saturated with phenolic resin, put under high pressure, and cooked until all the ingredients bond together into a single sheet of plastic.

In addition to the familiar varieties of laminate, there are some interesting recent variations. One of these is solid-core laminate, which doesn't have the kraft-paper core and corresponding dark line on its edge like regular laminate. Also available are decorative metal laminates. Although unsuitable for countertops, these laminates can

have almost mirrorlike finishes in metals like bronze, gold, copper, brass, and aluminum and are useful for unusual cabinetry designs. Wood-veneer laminates offer some exciting design options for cabinets and shelving. Laminates are even available as a flooring material.

Choosing laminate can be a bit overwhelming because there are so many choices in colors and textures. For countertops, at least, it pays to be a bit practical, since these surfaces can see considerable wear and tear. For example, matte finishes are preferable to glossy surfaces, which show scratches all too easily, or highly textured surfaces, which are more difficult to keep clean. Also, minor scratches in very dark colors appear to be white, because only the melamine top surface is affected. Darker colors also seem to highlight every speck of dust or errant glob of toothpaste.

One of plastic laminate's big advantages is price. Expect to pay about $1.00 to $3.50 per sq. ft. for uninstalled sheet goods. Pre-cut countertops in a limited number of styles and colors are a great bargain at your local home improvement center, typically costing between $5 and $10 per running foot. Custom-ordered and installed countertops begin at about $50 per running foot. Laminate flooring begins at as little as $3 per sq. ft.

2 Plastic laminate is a real workhorse when it comes to bathroom design. Durable, water-resistant, and available in an enormous variety of colors and patterns, plastic laminate can even conform to curved surfaces, such as this tub deck.

3 While not suited for use on countertops, wood-veneer laminates with a phenolic core combine the look and feel of natural hardwood veneers with the stability, durability, and workability of plastic laminate.

4 Although plastic laminate is most often used for countertops, it can also be used on other surfaces in the bathroom, such as the vanity cabinet shown here.

5 Wood-veneer laminates that have the appearance of a wide variety of species, grain patterns, and colors are available, offering new design possibilities for cabinetry and casework.

PAINT & WALLPAPER

1 The walls of a bathroom make a perfect canvas for this tumultuous *trompe l'oeil* wave mural. White Italian Abescato marble wainscoting and a custom ash cabinet inlaid with ebonized ash complete the composition.

PAINT AND PAINTING TECHNIQUES FOR BATHROOMS

Simply put, there's no other finish that can transform an interior as dramatically and cost-effectively as paint. A wonderful source of color and texture, paint can be applied by almost anyone with a minimal investment in time, tools, and materials.

The first step is to choose a primer that is specifically intended for the harsh conditions of the bathroom. The best primers inhibit vapor transmission, and some of them (like some bathroom paints) are treated with a mildewcide and stain killer. Primers that are intended for wood trim are different from primers that are intended for drywall surfaces.

Paint is decorative, but it should also be durable and cleanable. Flat paints have a high pigment-to-resin ratio, so they're good at hiding surface flaws and go on easily; unfortunately, they are almost impossible to keep clean. A better choice for often-scrubbed bathroom walls is gloss or semi-gloss paint, which has a higher resin-to-pigment ratio. Satin and eggshell-type paint formulations retain most of the cleanability of the high-gloss paints without the shiny look.

Alkyd (oil-based) enamels are generally more durable and abrasion-resistant than latex (water-based) enamels, but increasingly strict regulations regarding VOC (volatile organic compounds) content in paints and finishes have narrowed the performance gap. Latex enamels dry more quickly, clean up with water, and don't have an overpowering odor while they're drying. Paint that is intended for use on walls and ceilings should have a low-permeability rating, meaning that potentially damaging water vapor can't easily pass through the paint membrane.

Choosing paint colors can be both exhilarating and intimidating. Color chips and charts from the various manufacturers help, as do general color theory design guidelines (see p. 24). But in practice, there's nothing quite like seeing the actual paint in place in the bathroom. There, lighting conditions will show the paint in its true color and in relation to the other colors of the bathroom.

Besides experimenting with color, try some of the various decorative painting techniques. Stenciling is a relatively simple technique that was popular with colonial pioneers, particularly the Pennsylvania Dutch. Sponging, ragged finishing, and color-washing are other relatively simple techniques that can easily be mastered by amateur painters and which add subtle texture and color to ordinary wall surfaces.

2 This curved Art Deco vanity looks like maple but is painted yellow (with a camel overglaze) to match the walls. The marble countertop's greens and grays are also reflected in the leafy border painted on the mirror frame.

3 Decorative painting techniques like color-washing add a subtle stonelike texture and color to ordinary drywall surfaces.

4 Meticulously applied hand-screened wallpaper transforms this guest bath into a library; just don't try to take any of the books home with you. An antique marble countertop and antique silver sconces with new plaid shades lend a classic look to the composition.

BATHTUBS AND SHOWERS

Back in the "good old days," taking a bath meant dragging a wooden tub into the kitchen and filling it with hot water heated on the stove. No wonder bathing was only a weekly (if that) ritual. When a Wisconsin farm-implement manufacturer named John Kohler began enameling his horse troughs and welding legs to them around the turn of the century, a fixture, a company, and an industry were born. It wasn't long before indoor plumbing and dedicated bathrooms with tubs, sinks, and toilets were required in all new construction.

Now bathing and showering are integral parts of life. Many of us begin the day with an invigorating shower, not only because we need to get clean but also because it helps jump-start our bodies for the busy day ahead. Those who exercise at midday or in the late afternoon after work hit the showers again, or risk the disapproving looks of coworkers or spouses. And at the end of the day, or during weekend or vacation leisure time, many enjoy a longer soak in a hot sudsy bath, using that quiet time to ease the body and soothe the mind.

As you'll see in the following pages, tubs and showers have come a long way since the days of the weekly Saturday evening bath. Sure, we still use soap and water to get clean, but the advent of whirlpools, multiple showerheads, and hydromassage makes simple hygiene almost secondary to the simple pleasure that showers and baths now provide. More than ever, bathing and showering are just good clean fun.

SHOWER ENCLOSURES that are separate from the bathing area have become safer and more spacious. Custom-built enclosures use a variety of natural or synthetic materials to match the style of the bathroom, while manufactured acrylic and fiberglass units are economical and quick to install.

SHOWER VALVES AND SHOWERHEADS range from simple to spa-like. The single control/ single showerhead configuration shown here can be supplemented with track-mounted handheld showers and multiple body sprays.

BATHTUBS AND WHIRLPOOLS are great places to relax and unwind. While enameled cast-iron is a durable and traditional choice, larger tubs for two are available in acrylic or fiberglass.

TUB FAUCETS come in a number of styles and finishes, including this low-profile, high-volume Roman tub spout.

BATHING FIXTURES

1 Many bathrooms today have room for both a shower (here, situated in the corner) and a tub (hidden to the right). Glass block set into a grid in the ceiling above the showering and bathing area introduces natural light into this otherwise windowless interior bathroom.

2 Large walk-in showers without curtains or glass doors are easier to keep clean than smaller enclosures. A wall of glass block lets in light but maintains a bit of privacy.

THE TYPE OF TUB OR SHOWER you choose will depend on the space that is available and the kinds of use the bathroom receives. Where space is limited and full showering and bathing functions are required, manufactured fiberglass or acrylic combination tub/shower units are a good choice. Economical and easy to clean, they don't take up a lot of room, and many are available with whirlpool and spa features. When there's enough room in the bath, separating the showering and bathing functions is a good idea. Larger walk-in showers are safer and more comfortable to use, while soaking tubs can be set in more comfortable (and less waterproof) surroundings.

4 When space is at a premium, a combination tub/shower is a good choice, offering both showering and bathing functions while occupying a small footprint.

3 Tubs that are used for soaking rather than splashing can be placed almost anywhere. Here, an old enameled cast-iron freestanding tub is a perfect place to take a few moments to enjoy one of life's simple pleasures.

5 This frameless glass shower enclosure separates the shower and bathing areas, yet neither feels enclosed. The windows above the bath are conventional casement windows, while the shower window is fixed and waterproofed to prevent moisture damage.

2 Wood rafters overhead and a glass-block wall help transform a simple shower into an architectural space.

1 White pull-down shades transform this greenhouse-style glass sunspace into an intimate bathing area.

3 Even relatively small baths can have room for both a tub and a separate shower. The glass enclosure keeps the compact shower from feeling like a dark and confined closet.

4 The high eased back and gentle curves make this cast-iron clawfoot tub as comfortable as an old slipper.

5 Though better (and safer) for simple soaking, clawfoot tubs can be converted into showers with the addition of a vertical showerhead riser and a shower curtain ring overhead.

6 The unobtrusive frameless glass door has a minimal visual impact on this beautifully tiled combination tub/shower area.

7 Kids and pets can be popped into this mini-tub for a quick cleanup.

TUBS & WHIRLPOOLS

1 A molded-acrylic whirlpool tub is an inviting refuge for two in this French Country–style bathroom. The glazed ceramic tile on the planters, tub deck, and floor has the look of porous French limestone but is less expensive and easier to maintain.

PORCELAIN ENAMEL

Porcelain-enamel surfaces are durable, sanitary, easy to clean, and highly resistant to chemicals and corrosion. For many, there's no replacement for the solid quality of an enameled cast-iron tub, which is why decades-old clawfoot tubs that are in good shape are a valuable salvage item.

Porcelain enamel starts out as a mixture of minerals, such as silica, feldspar, and borax, which are heated into a molten state and then drawn out and cooled into a glasslike ribbon. The ribbon is pulverized to form "frit," the particulate sprayed onto the metal surface that is to be enameled. After the frit is sprayed onto the metal surface it is fired at a high temperature, which fuses it to the underlying metal, creating a durable coating that won't easily chip or peel.

Different types of metals can be coated with porcelain enamel, but cast-iron and steel are the two types you're most likely to encounter in the bathroom. Enameled-steel sinks were once popular because they offered a less-expensive and lightweight alternative to enameled cast-iron sinks. You don't see them much anymore except in junk yards because they proved to be prone to flexing and cracking.

Enameled-steel tubs are still manufactured, but they've been largely replaced in the marketplace by fiberglass and acrylic tubs. For the most part, vintage cast-iron fixtures, unlike old steel fixtures, are worth salvaging because they can be repaired or reglazed.

2 This freestanding cast-iron tub has a traditional feel yet is right at home in a contemporary setting.

2 Inspiration (and materials) can come from many sources. This old recycled cast-iron tub was found in a salvage yard and is set in a tub deck that's creatively tiled with both handmade tiles and blemished tiles from a local manufacturer.

3 This freestanding cast-iron tub has a traditional feel yet is right at home in a contemporary setting.

4 A salvaged clawfoot tub sits in a wooden deck with a removable frame-and-panel apron built around it. The tub sees only occasional use in this seasonal island home.

1 This bathing area has a Shaker-style simplicity. The wood tub deck requires more vigilance than a more water-resistant surface but can be adequately protected against moisture damage with a marine-type varnish.

2 Heavy cast-iron tubs have a lot of mass, which makes them quiet when water is running and helps to keep the water warmer during a long soak.

AN ACCESSIBLE TUB
Adding grab bars, a height-adjustable handshower, and transfer seating are easy steps to take and will make bathtubs safer and more accessible for everybody.

Height-adjustable handshower

Grab bars (side wall, 48 in. long, min.; end wall, 24 in. min.) are attached to re-inforced backing.

36 in.

9 in.

36 in.

Offset controls for easy access from both inside and outside the tub

Removable seat

Optional fixed seat

CHOOSING A WHIRLPOOL

Whirlpool tubs are available in a wide range of sizes, styles, and prices, so finding just the right tub can be a bit daunting. Here are some points to consider when choosing a whirlpool.

• Don't get a larger whirlpool than you need. Tubs can range in capacity from 50 gal. to almost 200 gal. While large tubs look great, they take a long time to fill and can tax even the largest hot-water supply system.

• Get right in the tub (with your clothes on, of course) at the showroom to try it out. Sitting in the tub will tell you if it is comfortable or not, and if it has enough room for you and your partner.

• Choose a quality acrylic tub rather than a lower-cost fiberglass unit. Acrylic tubs look better longer because their color won't fade, and you'll be able to buff out minor scratches.

• Choose the size and number of jets that will give you the type of massaging action you want. Large-diameter jets placed high on the tub walls produce a gentle swirling action, while smaller-diameter jets introduce a more vigorous massage to specific points on the body. Options like neck and back massage jets can be a godsend to those with chronic back problems.

• Consider an in-line heater. If you plan on taking a long bath, in-line heaters can maintain the water at a constant temperature for as long as you stay in the tub.

• Think about control options. Digital controls mounted right on the tub for easy access are the most convenient. Multi-speed and variable-speed pumps offer more flexibility than single-speed pumps.

3 This dramatic acrylic whirlpool is surrounded by glass and marble; an unusual cedar-lined light well through the ceiling provides a view of the stars. The skylight's clear $^3/_4$-in. glass lid doubles as a tabletop for the roof deck directly above.

4 Extending the tub deck provides shelf space for accessories, soap, and extra towels.

TUB/SHOWER COMBINATION UNITS

1 This one-piece acrylic tub fits into a standard 5-ft. bath alcove. The tub can be upgraded with options like multi-showerhead hydromassage and a whirlpool system.

2 Designed to fit into a corner without a walled enclosure, this whirlpool has room for two, as well as a freestanding tempered-glass shower enclosure with a sliding door.

3 A four-piece fiberglass combination tub/shower fits into a corner and offers a built-in seating area. When the unit is fitted with the roof cap and full-height shower doors, steam can be added for a soothing steam bath.

AN ACCESSIBLE SHOWER An adjustable-height handheld shower makes showering more comfortable for people of all sizes and abilities. Shower controls should be offset away from the water flow so that they can be easily operated from both inside and outside the shower.

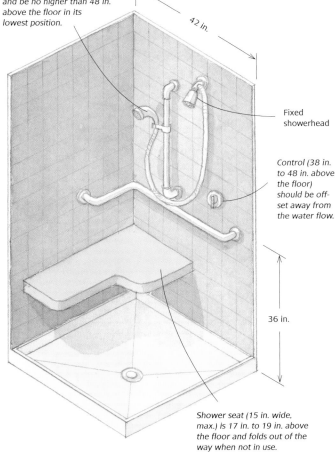

Handheld shower should be mounted on an adjustable track and be no higher than 48 in. above the floor in its lowest position.

42 in.

Fixed showerhead

Control (38 in. to 48 in. above the floor) should be offset away from the water flow.

36 in.

Shower seat (15 in. wide, max.) is 17 in. to 19 in. above the floor and folds out of the way when not in use.

4 Acrylic or fiber-glass tub/shower units that come in two or three pieces (like this one) can be maneuvered more easily through narrow halls and doorways, making them better for remodeling than bulky one-piece units.

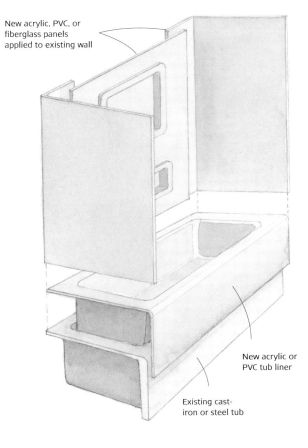

New acrylic, PVC, or fiberglass panels applied to existing wall

New acrylic or PVC tub liner

Existing cast-iron or steel tub

RELINING A BATHTUB
Tubs that are in need of repair or replacement can often be relined with a low-maintenance acrylic or PVC tub liner. the process takes less than a day and avoids the mess of demolition and construction.

R E N O V A T I O N   O P T I O N S

When renovating a bathroom, a major decision homeowners often face is whether to replace the tub. If the bathroom layout won't be changed, removing the old tub and gutting the room may not be necessary—an important consideration if alternative bathroom facilities are limited.

If the existing tub is an enameled cast-iron tub in reasonable condition, it may make sense to salvage it (either in its existing location or for use elsewhere). The expense of a new, high-quality tile or solid-surface surround may be comparable to the expense of replacing everything with an acrylic or fiberglass combination tub/shower unit. Keep in mind that chips and cracks in the surface of enameled tubs can be repaired and the entire finish of a tub in good working order can be reglazed on the premises.

Another option is to have an acrylic liner installed over your existing tub, and acrylic wall panels installed over the existing tile walls (see the drawing at left). This procedure typically takes about a day from start to finish and involves little demolition.

If you decide that the old tub must go, the first challenge will be to remove it. Old cast-iron tubs can be broken up into smaller pieces with a sledgehammer (be sure to wear eye and ear protection); old steel tubs have to be removed in one piece.

The second challenge will be to get the new combination unit in. Be sure to measure the doors and hallways of your house before deciding on a one-piece fixture; it may not fit into your house. In most cases, manufacturers offer comparable multisectional units that can be transported piece by piece and then assembled into a watertight unit on-site before installation.

MANUFACTURED SHOWERS

1 Manufactured shower units with matching glass doors are an economical alternative to custom-built showers. This corner unit is ideal for tight quarters.

FIBERGLASS VS. ACRYLIC

Most molded-plastic tubs and showers sold today are referred to as either fiberglass or acrylic. While acrylic units are manufactured of essentially the same materials and look identical to fiberglass units on the showroom floor, the difference is in the surface that you can see when the tub or shower is installed.

Fiberglass units start out on a mold that is first sprayed with a thin (1/64-in.) layer of pigmented polyester resin, called a gelcoat. Layers of fiberglass—a mixture of resins and chopped or woven glass fibers—are then added to the initial layer of gelcoat until it is about 1/8 in. thick. Before the unit is taken off the mold, various reinforcing "inclusions"—foam, wood, even corrugated cardboard—are added for structural rigidity.

Acrylic units start out a bit differently. First, a 1/8-in.-thick sheet of acrylic is heated, stretched over a tub or shower mold, then sucked into shape with vacuum pressure. After the acrylic shell cools, the fiberglass reinforcing and inclusions are added to give it strength and rigidity.

Besides cost—acrylic tubs are at least twice as much as comparable fiberglass models—you can usually distinguish acrylic units from fiberglass ones by their ceilings. Because they are vacuum-molded, acrylic shells need to be closed on all sides during the manufacturing process (though some manufacturers later remove the ceiling of some models). An acrylic tub or shower is more durable and harder to scratch than a comparable gelcoated fiberglass tub. Slight scratches in acrylic tubs can be sanded and buffed out; darker and brighter colors are less likely to fade.

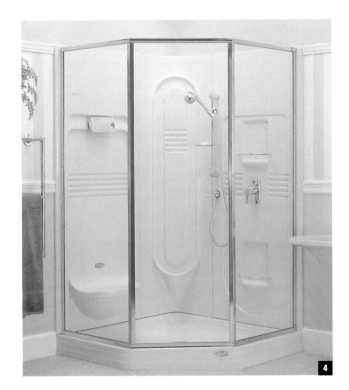

3 With a bubbling footbath and eight adjustable body and head hydromassage jets that can target specific muscle groups, showering becomes a head-to-toe massage. A recirculating pump maintains water pressure without depleting the water supply, while an in-line heater keeps the water hot.

2 This three-piece acrylic shower stall is perfect for remodels: It's leakproof and looks seamless. Getting a floor-to-ceiling model and an optional steam unit turns it into a steam shower.

4 Neo-angle showers utilize corner space efficiently and are available in different sizes. Many manufacturers offer options to customize the shower, such as the molded seat and waterfall showerhead shown here.

5 Neo-round showers are available in one-piece and multipiece configurations. The matching sliding door on this acrylic shower won't drip water on the floor when open.

CUSTOM SHOWERS

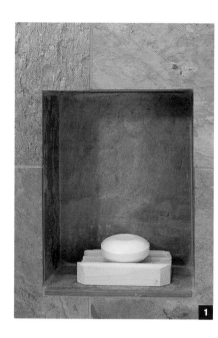

1 A recessed soap dish is an elegant detail in a tiled shower.

2 The curbless design, extensive use of granite, and frameless $^3/_8$-in. clear-glass enclosure make this shower feel less like a separate enclosure and more like a simple extension of the room. The four large custom-cut granite tiles that slope toward the shower drain were lightly scored in a grid pattern before installation and then grouted to improve traction.

3 This compact shower is well integrated with the whirlpool-tub deck.

4 Steps from the adjacent soaking tub lead down to this doorless shower and act as a curb to keep water in. Skylights overhead provide natural illumination.

5 Uncontrolled moisture and humidity can cause mildew to grow and wallpaper to peel, but this full-height glass enclosure keeps moist air in the shower, where it is efficiently removed by a combination ventilation fan/light. The shower seat folds down and out of the way when not needed.

5

FAUCETS AND SPRAYS

1 The polished-chrome finish on the tub valve has a traditional look that complements the clawfoot tub, while the handheld shower offers practical versatility.

2 Mounting a handheld shower on an adjustable track accommodates users of all sizes and matches the fixed showerhead.

3 Body sprays often have adjustable spray patterns, are typically located at shoulder, waist, and thigh height, and offer cleansing and therapeutic massage to all parts of the body.

SELECTING FIXTURES for a tub or shower isn't as simple as it used to be. Fixed showerheads are often supplemented with track-mounted handheld showers that accommodate short and tall users. Many showers now have multiple sprays that offer cleansing and massaging action directly to the body; you don't even have to get your head wet anymore when you take a shower. And control valves are safer, more stylish, and more reliable than ever.

5 This low-profile (but high-volume) waterfall spout doesn't get in the way of the spectacular view but fills the tub quickly with a cascading sheet of water.

6 Shower controls should be located away from the direct shower stream but within easy reach from either inside or outside the shower. Mounting showerheads and body sprays on opposing or adjacent walls provides more versatility for multiple users.

7 A handheld shower mounted on an adjustable track is more versatile than a fixed showerhead and can be adjusted to user height. The flexible extension hose makes it easy to clean the interior of the shower.

4 Preplumbed acrylic wall panels, complete with mixers, diverters, multifunction showerheads, and body massage jets, are available in a number of different configurations from many different manufacturers and can be used to quickly customize a shower.

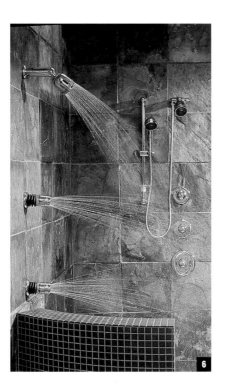

2 Less is sometimes more: a simple single-lever shower control and fixed showerhead.

1 Most manufacturers offer coordinating tub, sink, and shower valves and faucets with different finish and handle options.

3 This large shower has plenty of room for matching his-and-hers showerheads. Placing the handheld shower near a bench makes shaving legs more convenient.

4 For the true sybarite, what could be better than a cascading waterfall digitally controlled by a thermostatic valve and ten massaging body jets?

POLISHED CHROME is still a popular finish for bathroom fixtures because it is durable and easy to clean. Underneath the chrome, however, the best fittings are still made from corrosion-resistant machined brass. Molded-plastic and cast pot-metal plumbing fixtures with chrome finishes may have the look of their more expensive counterparts, but they won't offer the same performance and won't last nearly as long.

5 This limestone-tiled shower has an elegant yet efficient layout, with controls located near the door-less entry, a handheld shower within reach of the seating area, and a recess for soap and shampoo.

ANTISCALD SHOWER VALVES

Picture this: You're taking your morning shower, absentmindedly thinking about the day ahead while shampooing your hair. Unknown to you, someone elsewhere in the house flushes a toilet or starts the washing machine. This drops the house's cold-water pressure and sends a sudden surge of hot water out of the shower-head directly onto your head. Startled, you reflexively step back out of the shower stream but slip on the soapy side of the tub and start to fall. With nothing to grab onto but the shower valve, you inadvertently pull it all the way over to the hot side as you're falling, getting a full blast from your hot-water system's 140°F water. If you're lucky, you'll escape with only a few bumps and bruises and some scalded skin. Not a great way to start the day.

Scenarios like this have prompted national and local building codes to require (and manufacturers to produce) antiscald shower valves that help prevent injury in the bathroom. These valves work, so if you're remodeling a bathroom, plan on replacing your old shower valve with a new antiscald valve. And if you're building a new bath, you probably won't have a choice, because antiscald valves are now required in most new construction.

Pressure-balancing valves are the most widely available (and least expensive) type of antiscald valve. They work by detecting sudden pressure changes between the hot- and cold-water supplies and automatically compensating for them. Piston-type pressure-balancing valves have a metal cylinder that connects the hot and cold side of the valve. When the pressure drops on one side, the piston moves and reduces the flow of water on the other side. These valves are slightly noisier and more expensive than diaphragm-type valves, but both work in essentially the same way.

Thermostatic shower valves are a more expensive option. They contain a temperature-sensing mechanism that enables them to maintain a constant water-output temperature regardless of the temperature or pressure of the hot- and cold-water supplies. These valves can often be set to a preselected temperature, so that they operate at a predictable and comfortable water temperature. Some manufacturers also offer combination valves that react to both water pressure and water temperature.

It pays to spend a little more for a good antiscald valve. While there are plenty of inexpensive valves available, they don't all perform equally. The better ones react more quickly and smoothly to pressure and temperature changes, offer more options like preprogrammed temperature and volume control, and are more reliable. Although the cost of one of these shower valves may seem high, it is cheap insurance against burns and injury.

1 The contemporary look of the white single-handle shower valve, body sprays, and showerhead goes well with this dramatic glass-block shower stall.

2 Sometimes called a shampoo showerhead, this large high-volume, low-pressure overhead brass showerhead has an antique look and provides a soft but drenching flow of water.

OPTIMIZE YOUR SHOWER

Conventional wisdom doesn't always produce the most efficient or comfortable shower. For example, most showers have their controls located in the wrong place: directly beneath the fixed showerhead. A better location is offset toward the shower entrance and between 40 in. and 50 in. off the floor, so that the water can be turned on and adjusted from both inside and outside the shower. That way, you don't have to be immersed in cold or hot water to turn the shower on or off.

Similarly, there is nothing wrong with a single fixed wall-mounted showerhead...as long as everyone who uses it is the same height. For tall people, short people, and children, a handheld showerhead mounted on an adjustable track is a better idea. This kind of showerhead can be moved up and down so that users can keep their heads out of water. Hand-held showers with an extension hose are also more convenient for washing small children, pets, and the interior of the shower. Mounting a fixed showerhead on one wall and a track-mounted handheld shower on an opposing wall makes a shower more comfortable and versatile for multiple users.

Body sprays are typically mounted at shoulder, waist, and thigh level and are often controlled by a separate shower valve. The spray patterns and volume of individual body jets are usually adjustable and can vary from a soft spray to an invigorating massage. A body mist is a single metal bar with a series of jets in it that offers a gentler action than body sprays. One advantage of both body sprays and body mists is that you can take a shower without getting your head wet.

3 Many different styles of tub faucets—ranging from traditional to contemporary—also include a handheld personal shower, useful for washing hair and for cleaning up the tub afterward.

4 Water falls like rain from this jumbo-sized pool-house showerhead.

5 Sheet-flow tub faucets eliminate the awkward (and potentially dangerous) spout of traditional tub faucets.

6 Most manufacturers now offer lifetime-guaranteed polished-brass finishes for their tub and sink faucets. These finishes are virtually as scratch, tarnish, and corrosion resistant as polished chrome.

7 Though not quite as durable as polished chrome, this white epoxy-coated finish has a clean and contemporary look.

BESIDES POLISHED CHROME, there are other user-friendly faucet finishes. Polished brass has a beautiful look, but until recently the epoxy or lacquer coatings that were used to protect it were prone to damage from the abrasive cleansers typically used in the bathroom. Now most manufacturers use a new coating process and guarantee their brass finish for the life of the fixture. Nickel, pewter, and even gold are other metal finishes, each with a varying degree of resistance to scratching and corrosion. Colored epoxy-coated finishes are also available and give faucets and sprays an exciting contemporary look.

TOILETS
AND SINKS

Although tubs and showers receive the lion's share of attention (and money) in most bathrooms, toilets and sinks are the fixtures that do the dirty work day in and day out. Yet these fixtures and the rooms that contain them are a relatively recent development in the modern world. A century ago, indoor plumbing was a novelty; two centuries ago, it was virtually non-existent. At most, a fashionable mid-19th-century residence might have had a chamber pot or a portable toilet, a washbowl, and a closet in which to store these items.

Major cities, like London and Paris, began to develop sewer systems in the late 18th century to help dispose of waste and control disease. But it wasn't until the late 19th century that functional toilets started to become widely available. Building codes in the United States finally began to require bathrooms and indoor plumbing shortly after the end of World War I. So, over the course of a couple of decades, around the turn of the 20th century, the modern bathroom—a separate room with a toilet, sink, and a tub—was born. And if you doubt the widespread cultural impact of this change, try to imagine life without indoor facilities.

While current toilet, sink, and faucet designs are rooted in the past, new technologies and greater environmental awareness have resulted in fixtures that simply work better. As you'll see, toilets offer more features, are generally more efficient, and use less water, while sinks and faucets are now available in a wider array of shapes, styles, and materials than ever before.

FAUCETS are available in a number of different styles and finishes, ranging from traditional to contemporary. This single-control faucet has a durable polished-chrome finish and matches the horizontal-spray faucet mounted on the bidet.

SINKS are often the visual centerpoint of a bathroom, so they need to look good. Because they see considerable use, they should also be constructed of durable materials that are easy to clean.

BIDETS aren't an essential fixture, but they can be a useful addition to a bathroom. Bidets are usually matched with a similarly styled toilet, like these expensive wall-hung units.

TOILETS are now required to flush with a low, 1.6-gal. volume of water. This wall-mounted rear-discharge toilet has a concealed tank and is representative of the innovations that have improved the looks and performance of this prosaic fixture.

Toilets and Bidets

1 Set side-by-side in the privacy of their own alcove, a close-coupled two-piece toilet and matching bidet are separated by a strategically located, floor-standing toilet-paper holder.

2 Toilet tanks were once mounted high on the wall to increase water pressure in low-pressure systems and to enhance flushing efficiency. This model only looks old-fashioned; the toilet is actually a conventional 1.6 gpf (gallons per flush) model.

3 Toiletries and cleaning supplies are conveniently located close by this close-coupled toilet both in the shallow cabinet under the sink and in the wall-mounted cabinet above it.

THE FIRST TOILETS developed in the mid-19th century had a few flaws. For one thing, they tended to leak dangerous methane sewer gas back into the home, sometimes with explosive results. It wasn't until the vitreous-china toilet was developed by Englishman Thomas Twyford in 1885 that the modern toilet began to take shape. And it took another Englishman, Thomas Crapper, to patent and produce a reliable water closet that received widespread acceptance. American servicemen returning home from duty in England after World War I brought with them a new nickname for these new toilets, as well as a new appreciation for indoor plumbing.

4 Part of a suite of coordinated fixtures that includes a tub and a bidet, this two-piece toilet and matching sink have a traditional look yet are right at home in a modern bathroom.

TOILET OPTIONS

2 Popular two-piece toilets like Kohler's Wellworth flush efficiently, are widely available and inexpensive, and are at home in both contemporary and traditional-style bathrooms.

1 A triangular tank allows the toilet to be tucked into a corner, making access easier when floor space is at a premium.

3 The subtly sculpted lines of this traditional-looking two-piece toilet and matching bidet (right foreground) add a premium to their price but also a stylish touch to the bathroom.

4 At 16¹/₈ in. high, this ADA-compliant toilet is 2 in. taller than a standard toilet, making wheelchair transfers easier.

5 The elongated bowl of this Kohler Revival toilet is about 2 in. longer than a round-bowl toilet, a feature that is preferred by most users. Note the top-mounted pull-knob flush actuator.

6 Space-saving, shorter, round-bowl toilets are a good choice when floor space is limited. Some claim that the bowl's round shape enhances the toilet's flushing action.

They don't make toilets like they used to. But contrary to what you might have heard, this is good news. While there are those who would like to see a return to the days of water-guzzling toilets that can flush almost anything down the drain (along with up to 7 gal. of water with every flush), new toilet designs are more functional and efficient than ever before. And best of all, they save water, putting less stress on water supplies, private septic systems, municipal treatment plants, and ultimately on the environment.

First, a little background. Back in 1992, the National Energy Policy Act was enacted, which required that all residential and commercial toilets use 1.6 gal. of water or less per flush (gpf). Frankly, many toilet manufacturers were not quite ready for this new low-flush benchmark. Early attempts to meet federal requirements were often little more than band-aid approaches: plastic dams in the water tank, or early-closing flappers, for example. These "new" designs were actually old designs that now had to function using less than half as much water. So the early 1.6 gpf toilets earned a reputation (often well deserved) as poor performers that clogged easily and required double-flushing.

Necessity—and the law—is the mother of invention, however. To meet the new laws and satisfy consumers, manufacturers have scrambled to improve their toilet designs with refined hydraulic engineering and a number of innovations. For example, some toilets now use compressed air to compensate for the decreased water volume. Supplied either by a self-contained electric compressor or by a pressure tank that is charged by the pressure in a home's water supply, these toilets use the extra air to blast waste down the drain. More expensive than conventional toilets, these toilets are also considerably noisier.

Pressure-assisted toilets are a good choice for homes with old plumbing. Modern small-diameter plastic drain pipes have smooth interiors and just don't need a very large volume of water to move waste through them. Older 4-in. and 6-in. cast-iron drain pipes have a rough interior, and the flush from a 1.6 gpf toilet barely gets the inside of the pipe wet, much less move solid waste. While the air pressure helps move things along, it might also help to have high-use items, like a washing machine or shower, sharing the same drain line to help increase water volume.

The principles behind gravity-flush toilets, which account for about 90% or more of the U.S. market, have changed little since they were first introduced a century ago. Pushing the handle opens the flush valve, and water in the tank flows down into the bowl through holes in the rim of the toilet or through a siphon jet across from the drain (or a combination of both). This influx of water pushes the old water and waste through the trapway and down into the drain.

Manufacturers have enhanced the performance of gravity-flush toilets by tinkering with the size and shape of the bowl and trapway, by improving the trapway glazing, and by refining the siphon/vacuum action of the flush. Because they are simpler than pressure-assisted toilets, gravity-flush toilets are more reliable and less expensive, and they have a quieter flushing action.

Among the other improvements made to low-flush toilets is an increase in the size of their "water-spot," or the surface area of water in the toilet bowl. Larger water-spots result in a cleaner bowl. Some low-flush toilets also feature water-saving dual-flushing modes, with a lower 1.1 gpf flush as well as a standard 1.6 gpf. Despite the improvements and efficiency of the new toilets, however, consumers need to recognize that a new attitude toward flushing—and a plunger—are now a part of life.

AN ACCESSIBLE TOILET Most toilets are only 14½ in. high, which is a little too low for those who have difficulty sitting down and standing up. Higher, 16-in. toilets are available, while grab bars make toilet use easier and safer for everybody.

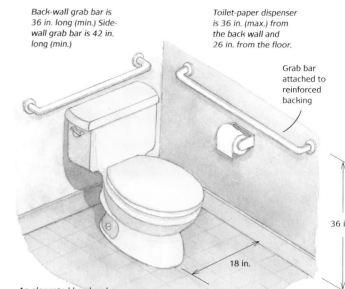

Back-wall grab bar is 36 in. long (min.) Side-wall grab bar is 42 in. long (min.)

Toilet-paper dispenser is 36 in. (max.) from the back wall and 26 in. from the floor.

Grab bar attached to reinforced backing

36 i

18 in.

An elongated bowl and a 16-in. seat height make access easier and more comfortable for wheel-chair users.

1 With a low profile, an easy-to-clean skirted design, and a heated seat, this one-piece toilet has a sleek and contemporary look that is also practical.

2 This ornately sculpted two-piece toilet has a Victorian charm that fits the romantic surroundings of the bathroom.

3 When you'd like a bidet but there's no room for another fixture, a personal-hygiene system that mounts like a toilet seat might be a good choice. This model features two electronically controlled self-cleaning bidet nozzles and a warm-air dryer.

4 One-piece toilets have a low profile and a sleeker, more contemporary look than comparable two-piece toilets. Because they are more difficult to manufacture, they are also more expensive.

6 If your tastes tend toward the unconventional, then this toilet and matching bidet might be just for you. The toilet has an integral electric pump and features a dual 1.1 gpf/1.6 gpf flushing capability.

5 Though white is a popular fixture color that never goes out of style, this expensive black low-profile one-piece toilet makes a dramatic statement. A small internal compressor supplies air pressure to improve the flush.

1 While clear window glass might make the user of this one-piece toilet feel exposed, frosted glass illuminates the space and obscures the view.

2 Wall-mounted toilets, like the Kimera by Absolute/American Standard, discharge to the rear rather than through the floor. The toilet's tank is hidden inside the wall, making the flush quieter; the toilet height adjustable.

3 A hidden exhaust system operated by and infrared sensor automatically pulls air containing odors and bacteria back through the rim holes of this toilet and out of the bathroom.

Let's face it: The bar has been raised on our bathroom expectations. Where simple tubs and showers were once enough, now we need whirlpools, hydromassage, and steam. So it's little wonder that we now expect more from our toilets than a simple flush.

At the same time that manufacturers are wrestling with the performance of their low-flush toilets (see the sidebar on p. 95), they've also come up with some interesting innovations. For example, electrically heated toilet seats are relatively common now, a feature that many will appreciate on a cold morning. Some specialty toilets have hydraulically operated seats that lift and lower automatically, a useful feature for elderly and disabled users who have difficulty getting up from a seated position. Another new feature is a soft-closing seat system that prevents toilet seats from slamming down onto the toilet accidentally.

Another seat innovation is a mechanism from Kohler called the Peacekeeper. Toilets fitted with Peacekeeper technology have no levers or buttons to flush the toilet but rely instead on the seat being lowered after use. Hence, the name. (Now, if they could only come up with a system that would clean the toilet automatically.)

Actually, the new personal hygiene systems are automatic cleaning systems, but they clean the body instead of the toilet. Basically an alternative to a bidet, personal-hygiene systems come in different configurations ranging from add-on toilet seats to self-contained toilets with shower/bathing functions. They work by directing a warm stream of water through a handheld wand or an automatically retracting nozzle toward the pelvic region. Some also provide an automatic air-drying function.

For example, Geberit offers the ShowerToilet, a complete toilet/bidet system that can be either floor or wall mounted. There's a retractable self-cleaning nozzle with an adjustable-intensity spray, as well as a warm-air dryer and air purifier. While this system isn't cheap, it probably is comparable to the cost of installing a high-quality toilet and bidet side-by-side, and it takes up much less room.

Panasonic and Toto offer add-on seats that mount on a conventional toilet and have many of the same features as the Shower-Toilet. The Toto Zoë has a similar spray mechanism, a seat-warming mechanism, and a small electric fan with a filter to help clear the air after use. Panasonic's IntiMist has twin cleaning nozzles, a heated seat, and a warm-air dryer. All of these units have a seat-contact safety switch that prevents the unit from operating accidentally, so that you won't get sprayed in the face while cleaning the toilet.

Relatively common in overseas markets, skirted toilets have only recently been introduced to the U.S. They feature a shroud or skirt that covers the trapway, resulting in a smooth base that doesn't have the dirt-collecting recesses of a conventional toilet. They also have a big footprint, sometimes eliminating the need for new flooring during renovation work.

If you're building a vacation home far from a municipal sewer system, you may be interested in composting or incinerating toilets. There are a number of different types of composting toilets available, but they all function basically like the compost pile in your backyard: Mix a carbon-rich material like sawdust with a little human waste and let it set for a while. Some smaller self-contained composting toilets also include a heating mechanism, which speeds the composting process. Larger-capacity systems usually consist of a simple toilet and a larger separate composting unit that is located directly beneath the toilet (usually in a basement). These systems also require venting and usually include a fan to draw odors away from the unit. Another type of self-contained toilet uses electricity to incinerate waste.

4 If there are a lot of boys in the family, a home urinal that's hard to miss and easy to clean might be the answer.

5 In addition to its bidet-like washing capability, Toto's friendly-looking Zoë personal hygiene system has an automatic air deodorizer.

6 A glass-block half-wall separates a one-piece toilet from the rest of the bathroom.

BIDETS

1 With a simple single-control horizontal-spray faucet on the bidet and a concealed tank on the matching toilet, this wall-mounted duo has a minimal presence and is easily cleaned.

1

2

2 In this spacious bathroom, the traditionally styled bidet is a hygienic complement to the matching two-piece toilet. Bidets and toilets are often available as part of an ensemble, with matching sinks and tubs.

BIDET-VALVE OPTIONS

While toilets are (for the most part) surprisingly affordable and quick and easy to install, bidets are not. This is because bidets aren't standardized like toilets; drain styles, locations, and configurations vary from bidet to bidet and from manufacturer to manufacturer. Bidets also require something that toilets don't: a valve to turn the water on and off. So when you choose a bidet, you'll need to decide at the same time the type and style of bidet valve that you want.

The simplest and least expensive type of bidet valve is the deck-mounted horizontal-spray bidet faucet (see the top left photo, facing page). This valve is similar in design and function to a standard sink faucet and mounts on the back of the bidet. When turned on, water sprays out from the valve spout only, though a pop-up stopper in the fixture itself can be used to retain water in the bowl. Bidet faucets can have either a single or double control.

Vertical-spray bidet valves are a bit more complicated. Fresh water from the mixing valve is sprayed from a sprinkler, or "rose," located in the bowl of the fixture, so these valves require a vacuum breaker (the drumlike or cylindrical metal contraption located near the back of some bidets) to keep contaminated water from back-siphoning into the fresh water supply (see the photo at right, facing page). Depending on the style of the fixture, this type of valve can be mounted either on the deck of the bidet, like a horizontal-spray faucet, or in the wall behind the fixture.

3 Horizontal-spray bidet faucets like this white single-control faucet are available in styles and finishes to match sink faucets.

4 Some vacuum breakers mount directly on the fixture itself. This contemporary bidet faucet features polished-chrome finials topped with brass-accented lever handles.

5 The brushed-chrome finish and traditional lever handles of this center-set horizontal-spray bidet faucet suggest an early American influence.

6 Vertical-spray bidet faucets have a bowl-mounted sprinkler that requires a vacuum breaker (the cylinder between the bidet and the wall) to prevent waste water from siphoning back into the fresh-water system.

Sinks

1 Vitreous-china pedestal sinks are available in a number of different styles, including this unusual double sink.

2 A pedestal sink has a small footprint and is a good choice for a compact bathroom.

3 A broad-shouldered pedestal sink has plenty of countertop room and fits in well with contemporary surroundings.

IF YOU THINK BATHROOM SINKS should be white, nondescript, and used primarily for brushing teeth, then you're in for a bit of a surprise. While classic white vitreous-china pedestals and enameled cast-iron drop-in sinks still rule the roost, there are plenty of other new styles, materials, and colors. Where under-counter storage and countertop space are important, vanity-mounted sinks remain a popular choice. Wall-hung sinks have experienced a resurgence in popularity, in part because they are the most accessible of the three types of sinks for handicapped users, but also because of new materials and innovative designs. And new interpretations of freestanding pedestal sinks contain at least a passing reference to tradition and can make a small bathroom feel more spacious and elegant.

4 This pedestal sink is simple yet refined, while the adjacent cabinet and counter-top provide needed and easily accessible bathroom storage.

4

5 An unusual cylindrical wood vanity with a round sink on top has the feel of a pedestal sink, but with storage space underneath.

5

6 With built-in towel bars, countertop space, and an offset white single-hole faucet, this pedestal sink's no-nonsense approach is perfect for this contemporary bathroom.

6

VANITY-MOUNTED SINKS

1 His-and-hers vanities have plenty of storage room, while raising the dramatic glass countertops provides a clear view of the stylish glass sink basins.

2 Lowering the sink slightly below the level of the vanity countertop and putting it into its own semi-circular island gives this small powder room an interesting visual twist.

3 Highly reflective surfaces—a stainless-steel self-rimming sink, polished-chrome plumbing, a corner-mounted glass countertop, and floor-to-ceiling mirrors—create a kaleidoscopic effect.

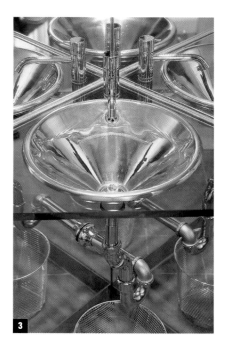

4 Mounting this sink bowl above the vanity rather than below it raises it to a more comfortable height while giving the maple cabinet a delicate and sculptural quality. The faucet is mounted through the mirror.

5 Sinks and countertops can be added to freestanding antique or contemporary furniture to give a bathroom an unfitted look.

SINK MATERIALS

When choosing a bathroom sink, consider the type of use it will receive. For example, powder-room sinks that are used only occasionally by careful guests don't need frequent or vigorous cleaning with harsh or abrasive chemicals. Family-bathroom sinks, on the other hand, are under almost constant use and abuse: toothpaste, cosmetics, nail-polish remover, sometimes even the paws and claws of a small dog or cat receiving an involuntary bath.

Vitreous-china pedestal and wall-mounted sinks have been an enduring choice for family baths and powder rooms for years. For one thing, they're virtually impervious to any kind of cleanser that you can throw at them. For a change of pace, take a look at one of the hand-thrown, custom-glazed ceramic sinks that are being produced by local potteries around the country. These sinks definitely don't look mass-produced, are quite resistant to most bathroom cleansers (though perhaps not to chips and cracking), and can add an unusual touch to a bathroom.

Enameled cast-iron sinks are still a popular choice, but don't confuse them with enameled stainless-steel sinks. Cast iron is quieter, tougher, and less apt to chip or crack. Brushed or polished stainless-steel sinks are not all that common in the bathroom, but their track record in the kitchen should make them good candidates if you don't mind their rather industrial look. These sinks are easy to clean and hide dirt well; the better-quality 18-gauge sinks with a higher nickel content are extremely stain- and corrosion-resistant. Other metals sometimes used for powder-room sinks include pewter and even silver, but these metals are softer and require considerable care to keep them from scratching.

Cultured-stone sinks that mimic the look of marble or granite have been around for years. Like other cultured stones, cultured marble is technically a cast polymer, created by mixing crushed marble with polyester resins, pouring the mixture in a mold, and curing it at room temperature. Some cultured-stone sinks are gel-coated to give the sink its color and texture. Inexpensive gel-coated sinks can crack and blister around the drain hole, while newer cast-polymer sinks have a higher percentage of harder materials like quartz and aren't gel-coated, making them more durable (and more expensive). And, of course, the stone-like qualities and workability of solid-surface materials make products like Corian an excellent and popular choice for sinks and combination sink/countertops.

WALL-HUNG SINKS

1 Many wall-hung sinks have exposed plumbing underneath, but this semi-pedestal model conceals the plumbing and provides protection for wheelchair users against scrapes and burns.

2 A granite wall-hung countertop provides a solid foundation for this delicate clear-glass bowl sink.

3 This spun-glass sink bowl is supported by a wrought-iron framework, but it can also be installed as a self-rimming sink in a counter or used freestanding above the counter.

4 This sink is made from iroko, a naturally rot-resistant African wood, that has been permanently stabilized through a special resin-impregnation process.

AN ACCESSIBLE SINK Wheelchair users need clear space beneath a sink for access to it; wall-hung sinks most easily meet recommended accessibility clearance requirements. Faucets with lever handles can be used by those with limited mobility in their hands, as well as by small children.

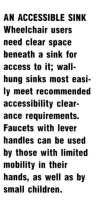

Mirror is tiltable, or extends down, so that the bottom is no more than 40 in. above the floor.

Lever handles are preferable to ball or cross handles.

Front of the sink should be 17 in. (min.) from the wall, and there should be 27 in. (min.) knee clearance beneath the sink.

Hot and cold supplies are shielded to prevent inadvertent contact.

5 The wall-hung sink in this Mediterranean-influenced powder room was carved from a block of Italian Pavus gray marble and shipped to the United States in two pieces. The walls were painted with a mottled faux finish to give them the look of old stone.

PLANNING AN ACCESSIBLE SINK

Sink planning doesn't have to be radically altered to accommodate the needs of the physically disabled, but there are a few ways that conventional sinks can be made more universally accessible. The first is to pay attention to the height of the sink. Most bathroom sinks are mounted about 30 in. above the floor, which is a good height for use by those in a seated position. Most standing adults really are more comfortable with a sink that is a bit higher, in the 36-in. to 38-in. range (the height of the average kitchen countertop). If there is room for two sinks, many universal designers suggest mounting them at different levels,

so that there is both a high and a low sink. In addition, some sinks designed for universal access are height-adjustable, either with a motorized drive or a hand-cranked lift mechanism.

Wheelchair users also need room to approach the sink and room underneath the sink for their knees (at least 27-in. clearance between the front lower edge of a sink and the floor). Wall-mounted sinks are ideal for this purpose, and many are designed with shrouds to protect the knees of users from hot pipes or rough surfaces. Pedestal sinks have a reasonable amount of clear floor

space too, though the pedestal intrudes somewhat. In some cases, the same sink style is available in both pedestal and wall-mounted configurations.

One of the drawbacks of wall-hung and pedestal-mounted sinks is that they often have limited countertop room. Vanity-mounted sinks usually have ample counter-top space, but the cabinet beneath the sink makes it extremely difficult for those in wheelchairs to get close enough to the sink to use it comfortably. Suspending a countertop between two flanking vanities and leaving at least 30 in. of free space beneath the sink pro-

vides both kneespace and storage space. Countertops also don't need to be supported by a vanity; wall-mounted brackets can provide invisible support and open access beneath. Remember that protective shrouds are still needed for pipes and sharp edges.

When planning storage for a universally accessible bathroom, remember that the optimal height is between 15 in. and 48 in. off the floor. Also, the mirror above the sink should either extend all the way to the top of the counter or be tiltable so that a person in a seated position can use it.

FREESTANDING & PEDESTAL SINKS

1

2 The spare geometry of the rectangular white pedestal sink contrasts with the warm texture of the richly colored tile and wood in this Arts and Crafts–influenced bathroom.

3 Perfect for a couple using the bath at the same time, this pair of pedestals feature wood bases and deep basins.

4 The rounded bowl and fluted base of this pedestal sink give it a classical look in keeping with the traditional style of this bathroom.

5 The mirror and contemporary surroundings contrast nicely with the tarnished brass faucet mounted on an antique enameled-steel pedestal sink.

FAUCETS

2 Classic good looks and durability make polished chrome a perfect finish for a kid's faucet.

1 The wrist-blade handles on this faucet are not only stylish but also easier to operate than knob-style handles for those with limited hand strength or dexterity.

3 Mounted on the wall, these wide-spread polished-brass faucets are well out of the trajectory of toothpaste and soap scum.

4 A chrome finish, cross handles, and an unusual gooseneck spout give this ornate faucet a sophisticated look.

6 The tall gooseneck spout offers more clearance, making it easier to wash face, hands, and hair at the bathroom sink, while the widespread lever handles allow easy cleanup.

5 Mini-widespread faucets mount on standard 4-in. centers but can be more difficult to keep clean than other faucet styles.

7 Baked-on epoxy finishes offer a colorful and contemporary alternative to metallic faucets and are quite durable, though they don't stand up to abrasive cleansers as well as chrome.

THE FIRST THING most people see when they look at a faucet is the finish. But underneath the gleaming chrome or shiny brass, the best faucets—the ones that will last the longest and cause the fewest problems—are made of solid machined or forged brass. Before settling on a faucet finish and style, consider how the faucet will be used. For example, tall gooseneck-style spouts that can swivel out of the way make washing up at the sink much easier, while lever-style handles are easier to operate than round knob-style controls for those with limited hand strength.

1 Water splashes into this glass bowl sink from a minimalist wall-mounted single-control faucet, which is available with different-length spouts.

4 The unusual sink design and corner location make a single-control wall-mounted faucet the right choice for this bathroom.

2 For the ultimate in cleaning convenience, this single-control faucet has a small, round footprint and is mounted on a seamless integral sink/countertop.

3 Lever-handled single-control faucets can be operated with either a hand or a wrist, while ceramic valving provides smooth and reliable performance.

5 Whimsical cast-metal animal figurines embellish the handles of this mini-widespread stem faucet.

6 This faucet's easily operated scroll-like handles are stylish and functional, while its beautiful PVD polished-brass finish is as durable as chrome.

FAUCET FINISHES

Polished chrome has a long track record as a durable faucet finish that won't scratch or corrode. No matter how grimy chrome bathroom fixtures become, they clean up easily with water, a sponge, and some abrasive cleanser. In fact, chrome offers such great protection that most faucets—even those with a brass finish—have an underlying layer of chrome, which is electro-chemically deposited over a nickel plating.

Many people prefer the look of polished brass to chrome, but unprotected brass oxidizes when it comes in contact with air. Clear protective lacquer and epoxy coatings help control tarnishing, but they don't stand up well to abrasive cleansers. However, a new technology called physical vapor deposition (PVD) offers a shiny brass finish that has virtually the same durability as chrome. Different manufacturers call their PVD brass finishes by different names, but most of them offer lifetime warranties on the finish, which will likely replace other brass finishes currently available.

Colored-epoxy finishes are also popular, particularly in white. These finishes are baked on, durable, and easy to clean, though not as scratch-resistant as either chrome or brass. Abrasive cleansers should also be avoided with this type of finish.

7 A single-hole faucet is required for the integral faucet deck of this beautiful basin sink, which is made of clear white ¹/₂-in. Starphire glass etched with a frosted banana leaf design.

8 The spout of this faucet is actually a chrome shower nipple with a knotted plastic extension.

1 Water falls from the copper spout into a copper bowl. The body of this unusual faucet is brass.

2 White epoxy-coated finishes have a clean, contemporary look.

3 Polished-brass finishes using new physical vapor deposition (PVD) technology are virtually as durable as chrome and come with a lifetime warranty against tarnishing and corrosion.

CERAMIC-DISK CARTRIDGE FAUCETS Smooth and reliable performance is a hallmark of faucets with ceramic-disk cartridges. The ceramic disks used in these cartridges are nearly as hard as diamonds and are highly resistant to corrosion, chemicals, and mineral deposits.

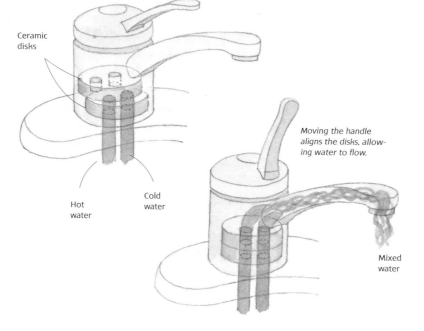

Ceramic disks

Hot water

Cold water

Moving the handle aligns the disks, allowing water to flow.

Mixed water

FAUCET VALVES

There are four basic types of faucet valves. Traditional stem faucets rely on **compression valves** to control the flow of hot and cold water. When the faucet handle is turned, a small rubber washer that seats against the bottom of the valve lifts and water flows. **Sleeve cartridges** were designed to replace compression valves and can be used in both single- and double-control designs. Although repair is quick, replacement cartridges can cost between $10 and $20, far more than the pennies needed for a new rubber washer on a stem faucet.

Ball valves are often found on single-handle faucets. A hollow ball with three holes—two for the hot and cold supplies and one leading to the spout—rotates within the faucet body; varying the position of the ball with the handle varies the alignment of the holes, changing the mix of hot and cold and the volume of the water.

State-of-the-art **ceramic-disk cartridges** are now widely used in both single-control and double-control faucets. The cartridges consist of two highly polished ceramic disks with small openings through which water flows. Rotating the disks moves the holes into or out of alignment, increasing or decreasing the flow of water through the cartridge (see the drawing at left).

FAUCET STYLES
Faucets fall into one of to broad categories: those that have separate controls for hot and cold water, and those with the temperature and volume controlled by a single handle. Tall spouts are more functional than low ones, while lever-type handles are the easiest to operate.

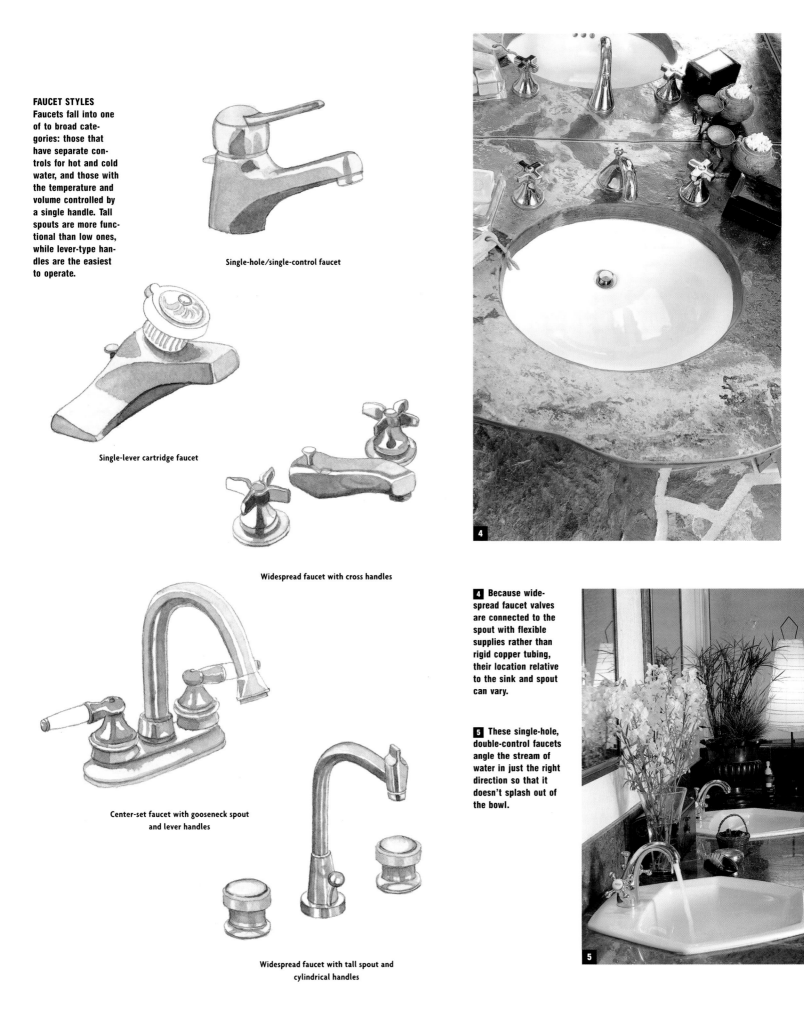

Single-hole/single-control faucet

Single-lever cartridge faucet

Widespread faucet with cross handles

Center-set faucet with gooseneck spout and lever handles

Widespread faucet with tall spout and cylindrical handles

4 Because widespread faucet valves are connected to the spout with flexible supplies rather than rigid copper tubing, their location relative to the sink and spout can vary.

5 These single-hole, double-control faucets angle the stream of water in just the right direction so that it doesn't splash out of the bowl.

STORAGE SOLUTIONS

One of the remarkable things about old houses is their limited storage, as if the people who lived in them owned only the clothes on their back and a few other possessions. Of course, they used alternative storage systems—wardrobes, chests, and bureaus, for instance. Perhaps more important, they just didn't have as much stuff that needed to be stored.

"Stuff" is at the heart of the matter when talking about modern bathroom storage. Medicine, tooth-care items, shaving gear, soap and shampoo, cosmetics, first-aid supplies, hair dryers, cleaning products, and towels and washcloths are among the items that need a home. Some items are used often, while others are used infrequently; some are quite small, others are rather bulky. Ideally, your bathroom storage system will provide a place for everything that's quickly and easily accessible, whether the bathroom itself is spacious or compact.

Cabinets are the basic components of bathroom storage. They offer an out-of-sight space for items of all shapes and sizes and can be fitted with drawers, shelves, tilt-out hampers, and other accessories to maximize their efficiency. Shelving is an often-overlooked form of bathroom storage and can either be enclosed in a cabinet or exposed to view. Strategically placed pegs, hooks, and towel bars are an indispensable part of any bathroom storage system. And as bathrooms become larger, there is more space for other storage solutions, such as freestanding furniture, closets, and extra cabinetry to hold linens, clothing, and exercise equipment.

UNDER-SINK STORAGE isn't all that convenient for frequently used items, but it's perfect for bulky items like cleaning supplies, large packages, and boxes. The curved fronts of these vanities help to soften the look of the bath's hard marble-tile floor, walls, and countertop and its rectilinear character.

A FULL-HEIGHT LINEN CABINET strategically located between the shower and the soaking tub is a handy spot for storing towels. The middle door above the open shelf conceals a television mounted on a sliding turntable.

SHELVING can be enclosed in a cabinet or open to view. Either way, it provides convenient storage for often-used items like clean towels and cosmetics.

DRAWERS offer access to items that need to be close at hand. In the bathroom, shallow drawers are better than deeper drawers, and they can be fitted with dividers and inserts to help keep everything organized.

CABINETRY

1 Contrasting decorative overlays and unusual pulls give the surface of this cabinet style and texture.

2 The deep cabinet space beneath a sink is often cluttered with plumbing and is difficult to reach, so it's best suited for bulky storage and cleaning supplies; the shallower flanking drawers are better suited for often-needed items.

3 Four small above-counter drawers are recessed into this bathroom's beaded wainscoting, providing quick access to cosmetics and tooth-care items from the twin sinks. Note the matching beaded panels in the cabinet doors.

MOST BATHROOMS need all the storage help they can get, and cabinets—whether freestanding or built-in—supply it. Vanities and medicine cabinets usually come to mind first when thinking about bathroom storage, but except in very small baths, the best place for storage isn't necessarily directly below or above a sink. In larger bathrooms, look for cabinetry that offers storage in the midrange, somewhere between knee and chin level. Cabinet-mounted drawers, shelves, and bins placed at this level next to a sink or on an adjacent wall offer the most accessible storage for the numerous small items that need to be kept close at hand in the bathroom.

4 Delicately contrasting green detailing on the molding of this painted and glazed curved-front vanity picks up the green of the marble countertop. An antique lantern hung overhead and two nickel-plated pole-mounted fixtures attached directly to the countertop provide light for the vanity area.

CABINET DOOR STYLES Different door styles are available for both frameless and face-frame cabinetry and can give them either a traditional or contemporary look.

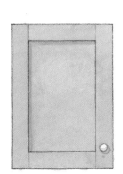

Frame and flat panel
(or mirror)

Flat (or slab) door with
J-channel pull

Raised panel

Curved raised panel

Mullion glass panel
(or mirror)

Ladder

Cathedral raised panel

Board and batten

2 A large floor-to-soffit frameless cabinet flanking a cherry-veneer vanity provides plenty of storage at all levels for everything from towels to medicine to toilet paper.

1 The countertop of this higher-than-normal vanity cabinet is 36 in. off the floor (rather than 31$\frac{1}{2}$ in.), making room for an extra pair of drawers and placing the sink at a more comfortable height for average-sized and tall users.

3 A painted charcoal-gray apron with routed panels hides the plumbing and bottom of the white under-mount sink, while an above-counter cabinet provides usable storage. In between is a Dakota mahogany granite countertop.

4 Traditional white-painted face-frame cabinetry with beaded raised-panel doors and drawers has a classic look. Many bathrooms also serve as dressing areas, and some designers like to dedicate vanity drawers and storage for underwear and lingerie.

VANITY OPTIONS

1 An example of unfitted cabinetry, this freestanding charcoal-colored bureau-style vanity stands in front of a large arched window wall. The vanity features Shaker-style frame-and-flat-panel doors and drawers.

1

2 New and unusual cabinet designs, such as this curved-front vanity, are possible with new laminate veneer materials.

3 A simple work table topped with a self-rimming sink and a slatted bottom shelf offers country charm with a twist of sophistication.

4 A place to sit is a convenient feature for the lady of this house. While the frame-and-panel doors give the cabinetry a traditional look, the cabinets are frameless.

FITTED VS. UNFITTED

A few years ago, English designer Johnny Grey popularized unfitted kitchens, composed of individual pieces of furniture-like cabinetry, each designed for a specific need. Recognizing the stylistic limitations of fitted kitchens—often monotonous banks of cabinets and unrelieved expanses of countertop—Grey deconstructs them into their working components (food prep, dishwashing, storage, cooking, socializing, for example) and then reconstructs them into functional and architecturally eclectic spaces.

Fitted bathrooms—a vanity tucked into an alcove or between two endwalls with a continuous countertop, for example—evolved out of the same design trends that resulted in fitted kitchens: Standardized cabinet sizes and plastic-laminate countertops result in a lot of storage bang for the buck. But while mass production and standard-sized rooms are efficient and economical, the resulting bathrooms all tend to look alike.

Unfitted bathroom cabinetry—whether in the form of a simple vitreous-china pedestal sink, a chest of drawers, or a sink dropped into a bureau—helps to reclaim a bathroom's individuality. When space is limited, an unfitted cabinet tends to draw attention to itself, rather than to the space surrounding it, creating the illusion of more room. Unfitted cabinetry can also be more eclectic, more task-specific, more personal, whether in a large or small bath.

Bathroom furniture can come from a number of sources. Old bureaus, commodes, and tables can be found almost anywhere—in flea markets or attics, at auctions, or in antique shops. New furniture-style cabinetry can now be found in many manufacturer's catalogs, or it can be commissioned at a local cabinet shop.

1 A central bank of drawers breaks up the expanse of cherry cabinetry and provides useful storage right where it's needed.

2 The corners of this vanity cabinet have been mitered to eliminate sharp edges, while slide-out wire baskets for storage are mounted inside on tracks. Though there are no drawers, the large countertop offers plenty of room for the soaps, jewelry, and cosmetics of the young girl who uses this bathroom.

CABINET CONSTRUCTION While frameless cabinets (left) offer slightly more accessible storage space and simplified construction, face-frame cabinets (right) have a more traditional look. A wide range of drawer and door styles is available for both types of cabinets.

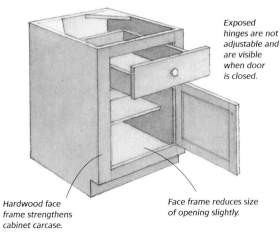

Adjustable hinges are concealed when door is closed.

Exposed hinges are not adjustable and are visible when door is closed.

Adjustable legs simplify installation but need finish trim.

Inside of cabinet is completely accessible when door is open.

Hardwood face frame strengthens cabinet carcase.

Face frame reduces size of opening slightly.

Frameless cabinet

Face-frame cabinet

Whether a cabinet is hand-crafted in a local shop or mass-produced in a factory, it will be put together in one of two ways. Traditional face-frame cabinets are actually lightweight boxes built out of sheetgoods—typically particleboard or plywood—and braced by a solid-wood overlay (the face frame) to which the doors are attached. European-style frameless cabinets are essentially heavier-duty boxes to which the doors and cabinet hardware are directly attached.

Face-frame cabinets evolved with the introduction of plywood earlier in this century, which gave cabinetmakers an economical and lightweight alternative to solid-wood construction. Hand-crafted furniture-grade cabinets, which are labor- and material-intensive, gave way to mass-produced plywood cabinets with standardized dimensions in the wake of the post–World War II housing boom. While these cabinets benefited (or some might say suffered) from less expensive materials and construction techniques in their boxes, they still needed their hardwood face frame to maintain the look of traditionally styled cabinetry and to give the cabinet strength.

Frameless cabinetry evolved in war-torn Europe at about the same time. Instead of a face frame, this style of construction relies on the box itself to give the cabinet structural integrity. For this reason, frameless cabinets are typically constructed of $^3/_4$-in.-thick sheet goods, sometimes a veneered plywood but more often medium density fiberboard (MDF) with a durable and easy-to-clean melamine finish.

A face frame on one of these cabinets would be redundant, since the box itself is rigid enough to mount all of the hardware directly to it. As a result, there is actually more usable space in a frameless cabinet, because the interior isn't partially blocked by a face frame and drawers can be made slightly wider, or almost the full width of the cabinet.

At one time, frameless cabinets had a decidedly European look: monolithic slab-type doors, concealed hinges, and pulls that are molded right into the door. And Euro-style hinges used on frameless cabinets were superior because they were stronger, adjustable, and offered more features. Now, however, the distinctions between frameless and face-frame cabinets have blurred. Both types of cabinets are available in either contemporary or traditional styles, and concealed Euro-style hinges are also available to fit face-frame cabinets.

3 The graceful curve of this cherry cabinet is uninterrupted by knobs or pulls, giving the contemporary vanity a clean and uncluttered look that contrasts nicely with the spider-black marble countertop.

4 Extending the green marble flooring up into the kick space makes these traditional frame-and-panel cabinets appear to be floating.

1 The warm wood tones of the naturally finished teak drawer fronts are a welcome interruption to the hard, industrial surfaces of this contemporary stone and stainless-steel vanity.

2 Maple has a clean, contemporary look and is a fitting material for this simple Shaker-style vanity.

3 The knotty-pine finish of this bureau-style vanity has a warm yellow tone that offsets the formal black-and-white flooring and dark wallpaper in this powder room.

4 A set of matching his-and-hers vanities is separated by a tall floor-to-ceiling cabinet. Made from aniline-dyed tay wood veneer, the cabinets are topped with a sandstone countertop.

5 The curves of this sleek contemporary cabinet are echoed in the mirror and high arched window, which has clear-glass shelving mounted in front of it.

6 Found at an antique store, this walnut buffet was recycled into an elegant bathroom vanity with the addition of a tile countertop, a protective urethane finish, and twin sinks.

MEDICINE CABINETS

1 Tall mirrored medicine cabinets mounted on a face-frame vanity flank a large central mirror. Beaded detailing and crown molding up-grade these cabinets to furniture status.

2 This medicine cabinet has glass-front doors and a country flavor. While the small shelf offers usable storage for soap and tooth-brushes, some might find the absence of a mirror distracting.

3 Recessed into the wall, this simple white medicine cabi-net offers effective storage and unobtru-sive counterpoint to the beaded wainscot-ing and wood and glass shelving in this 1930s-style bath.

4 A natural finish and window-style trim details on this recessed oak medi-cine cabinet empha-size its presence.

5 Although this tall medicine cabinet isn't recessed, its extended sides and continuous trim around the top make it look built-in. Note how the vanity cabinets vary in height so that the countertop can extend over the toilet for additional shelving and a storage drawer.

OTHER CABINETRY & STORAGE

1 Idiosyncratic furniture like this small glass-fronted cupboard can provide useful bathroom storage while adding an eclectic element to a bathroom.

2 Conveniently located between the sink and the tub, this large ash cabinet has a yellow-dyed finish and plenty of room for towels and other bath supplies.

3 Attractive and functional, this small freestanding cabinet has a marble top and flanks a pedestal sink.

4 Concealed behind doors and recessed into the wall above the toilet, these drawers and shelving take advantage of unused space without blocking access to the toilet tank.

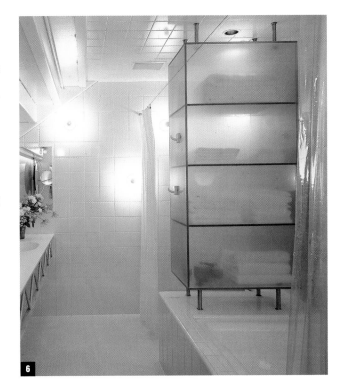

5 A blue sideboard-style cabinet adds colorful counterpoint, display space, and needed storage to this contemporary glass-and-chrome bathroom.

6 Poised between the tub and toilet, a translucent-glass closet stores towels and linens, while a white drape suspended from a cable provides additional privacy in the toilet area. A metal truss supports the long span of the Corian countertop.

STORAGE GUIDELINES
Efficient bathrooms feature a variety of storage solutions for the many different items that are needed there.

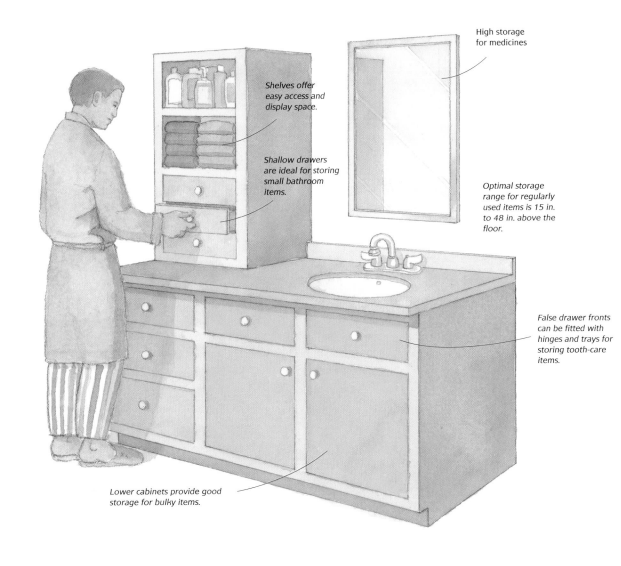

Shelves offer easy access and display space.

Shallow drawers are ideal for storing small bathroom items.

High storage for medicines

Optimal storage range for regularly used items is 15 in. to 48 in. above the floor.

False drawer fronts can be fitted with hinges and trays for storing tooth-care items.

Lower cabinets provide good storage for bulky items.

SHELVING AND SPECIAL STORAGE

1 Recessed into a marble-tiled tub alcove, glass shelving has a low profile and offers a highly visible place for collectibles.

CABINETS ARE JUST ONE PART of the bathroom storage equation. Shelving—either open to view or enclosed in a cabinet—is another way to add practical storage space to a bathroom. Shallow shelves are more practical than deep ones because items are less likely to get buried in the back, while adjustable shelves can be moved up or down to accommodate different-sized objects. Open shelves are the perfect place for brightly colored towels and decorative bottles and soaps. One drawback: Shelves collect dust, so plan on using enclosed shelves for things that don't get used much.

2 The view from the tub toward the aquarium is dramatic, and there's no shortage of storage for towels—but try finding a fish when you need one.

4 Crown molding tops off this bookcase-style shelf unit, while the large cabinets underneath offer additional storage.

3 Cabinet doors are useful for hiding clutter but can get in the way when storing items that don't need to be hidden from view. Open glass shelving above the vanity offers additional storage for cosmetics, bottles, and family photos.

5 Flanked by twin vanities, this window seat has storage underneath, with open bins for extra towels and pull-out bins for other supplies.

1 Recessing the open glass shelving into the wall near the tub helps keep the bathing area uncluttered and offers easy-access storage for clean towels and bathing accessories.

1

2 While a wood cabinet might block the view, these open shelves don't. Clean towels and accessories for the nearby pedestal sink are close at hand.

STOCK VS. CUSTOM

There are a number of different sources for bathroom cabinetry. Kitchen and bath stores, local lumberyards, building supply centers, and home improvement superstores carry a wide range of stock and semi-custom cabinetry, while local cabinetmakers offer custom-made cabinetry that can be built exactly to your specifications.

When comparing prices of custom cabinetry and stock or semi-custom cabinetry, be sure that you aren't comparing apples and oranges. Custom cabinets may offer better quality construction (dovetailed drawers, for example, or thicker cabinet carcases made out of plywood rather than particleboard) than seemingly comparable manufactured cabinets. And custom cabinets can have features like bins and drawers designed specifically for your bathroom. Custom cabinets can be built in shapes, sizes, materials, and finishes that

aren't available from the major manufacturers.

Don't assume that you can just go to a store and buy stock cabinetry. Because cabinets are bulky and take up considerable warehouse room, even stock cabinets usually need to be ordered; depending on the manufacturer, it can take up to six weeks or more for delivery.

At first glance, cabinets that carry Kitchen Cabinet Manufacturers Association (KCMA) certification look virtually identical. Stock or semi-custom, the cabinet parts that show—doors, drawer fronts, and face frames—are built and finished the same. The differences between the two begin to show up when you examine drawer and cabinet carcase construction. Better cabinets have drawers that are more ruggedly constructed out of thicker stock and carcases built out of sturdier plywood rather than particleboard.

3 A tall cabinet anchors this polished-concrete countertop while supplying needed storage in this contemporary bathroom. Note the additional storage beneath the counter.

1 Freestanding furniture like this glass-topped coffee table can be moved around in the bathroom to where it is most convenient.

2 Useful add-on accessories like this slide-out wire-basket laundry hamper optimize bathroom storage. Note the frameless cabinet style; the door swings completely out of the way, allowing easy access to the interior.

3 Doing away with the doors opens up these base cabinets, making it easier to grab a towel before heading off to the shower.

ACCESSORIES HELP CUSTOMIZE bathroom storage. A few manufacturers offer molded plastic inserts that slip into standard-sized drawers and help organize small objects like cosmetics and tooth-care products. A molded tray and special hinges can also be added to the false drawer fronts found on some vanities, offering a convenient place to put toothpaste and toothbrushes. And a number of different types of add-on wire-basket-type accessories are available, including tilt-out and pull-out hampers and sliding trays for holding cleaning supplies.

More often found in kitchens, appliance garages are a great place to store (and conceal) bulky but frequently used accessories like blow-dryers. Don't overlook pegs, hooks, and towel bars. Placing them in convenient locations around the bathroom could mean the difference between a clean floor and a messy one.

4 Though it takes up just a few square feet of floor space, this storage system features plenty of drawers, a tilt-out center bin, a countertop-level garage for often-used accessories, and a tall cabinet with double doors.

5 Closing this sliding tambour door quickly conceals countertop clutter. Note the convenient electrical outlet mounted in the wall of the appliance garage cabinet.

6 The look is antique to match the furniture in the rest of this Connecticut cottage home, but the convenience of a tilt-out hamper is decidedly modern.

LIGHTING, HEATING, AND VENTILATION

Most of us don't have to be sold on the idea of natural lighting: Sunlight streaming through a window simply makes us feel good. As a bonus, rooms with appropriately placed windows rely less on artificial lighting and are more energy-efficient. A good bathroom lighting plan will include as much outside window area (without compromising privacy) as possible. Unfortunately, the sun doesn't always shine. When it doesn't, turn instead to artificial sources for general illumination, task lighting, accent lighting, and nightlighting. Both windows and artificial lighting can be used to help create the ambiance of a bathroom and to positively affect the mood of the people using the space.

Bare wet skin is particularly sensitive to cold and drafts, so heating and ventilation should also be carefully considered in any bathroom design. New heating ideas, ranging from in-floor radiant heating to wall-mounted towel-warming radiators, offer stylish alternatives to traditional heating systems. And if an existing bath has a tendency to be chilly, options exist to supplement the heat, including combination ceiling fan/light/heaters and wall-mounted electric panel radiators.

The most energy-efficient way to ventilate bathroom odors and moisture is by opening a window. While operable windows are always a good idea in any environment, they aren't always a practical method of ventilation in winter. Plan on including a ventilation fan to get rid of moisture before it can start to peel your wallpaper or breed mold and mildew on your bathroom walls.

RECESSED-CAN FIXTURES are available with a number of trim options that allow them to distribute light in different ways, ranging from intensely focused to broadly diffuse. Best for general lighting, they're also used in this bath to illuminate the vanity area.

WINDOWS are available in a wide range of styles and sizes. Large glass-block windows contribute to the overall ambient light in this bathroom yet still allow the bathing area to feel secluded.

SKYLIGHTS can be a wonderful source of natural light in a bathroom because they don't compromise privacy; operable skylights can provide an efficient means of ventilation.

MIRRORS not only serve a functional purpose but also help to expand the feel of the interior space. Here, wall-to-wall mirrors over the countertop make the long corridor-like bathroom seem wider, while a smaller shaving/cosmetics mirror is mounted on a center cabinet.

LOOKING AT LIGHTING

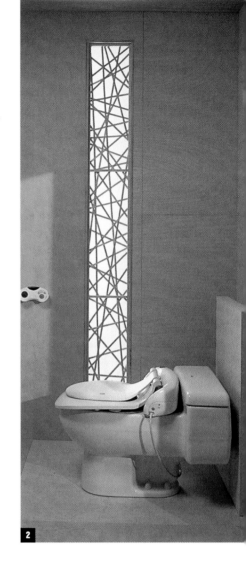

1 Daylight splashes through this double-hung window overlooking the Green Mountains of Vermont. A wall-to-wall mirror gathers and reflects light and the view, while the simple overhead fixture lights the vanity.

2 Muted natural light filtering through a tall translucent window contributes to the serenity of this bathroom.

3 Large windows offer more than a fleeting glimpse of Maine's tranquil Camden harbor, while operable skylights provide both light and ventilation. Twin heat lamps overhead warm up the toweling-off area.

WINDOWS NOT ONLY LET IN LIGHT but also keep us connected with the outside world. Choose a specific window type—casement or double-hung, for example—for the way it matches your home's architecture. But orient it on the wall or in the ceiling for the view, which will change with the time of day and with the seasons.

When the sun goes down and you turn on the lights, you should like what you see. Choose lighting fixtures that provide both general illumination and appropriate task lighting for applying cosmetics or shaving. Incandescent lamps offer warm light, but new color-corrected compact fluorescent lamps are considerably more energy-efficient and offer the same quality of light.

4 The natural daylight provided by the twin casement windows flanking the vanity area is ideal for applying makeup. Translucent glass overhead helps soften harsh shadows from the artificial light fixture.

5 Instead of a mirror reflecting inward, a window wall behind the vanity offers a view outside to the world beyond the glass. A heater located in the vanity's kick space warms the toes on cool mornings.

6 A diamond pattern in the tempered cast-glass windows distorts the view enough to provide privacy in this bathroom overlooking a golf course. Both general and task lighting are provided by a number of recessed fixtures, including a fluorescent fixture with a vapor-proof lens (required by code) in the shower area.

NATURAL LIGHTING

1 Salvaged from a London flea market, these leaded-glass windows let in plenty of natural light while tastefully and colorfully obscuring the view.

2 A small stained-glass window next to the tub depicts the larger view of Vermont's Lake Champlain that's visible through the big windows and skylight of this comfortable bathroom suite.

3 This tub/shower area is illuminated from above by an operable skylight; translucent glass block is geometrically interspersed with the tile in the back wall and tub apron.

BATHROOM LIGHTING

Task lighting is typically located near the vanity area but is sometimes a bathroom's primary general lighting source as well, particularly in small powder rooms. Many bathroom vanities have overhead lighting supplied either by fixtures mounted in a soffit or by a fixture above the mirror, but this doesn't provide the best source of light. Grates and diffusers can help soften the overhead shadows, as can multiple lamps, which spread the light over a wider area. The best solution, though, is to mount light bars with multiple frosted lamps on the wall at about eye level and on either side of the mirror. Called vertical cross-illumination, this type of lighting scheme approximates daylighting, reduces glare, and softens harsh and distorting shadows.

General lighting, needed in larger bathrooms, is found in the form of wall- or ceiling-mounted fixtures or recessed-can fixtures. As a rule of thumb for ceiling-mounted fixtures, plan on 1 watt of incandescent light per square foot of floor area. Recessed light fixtures need at least twice that wattage to achieve the same amount of illumination, while fluorescent fixtures require about one-third to one-half the wattage of incandescent fixtures.

Accent lighting can be used to highlight an area or an object for dramatic effect. Placed in the toekick area of a vanity cabinet, it can make the cabinet appear to float. Providing dimmer controls for all types of bathroom lighting allows you to sculpt the bathroom's mood, from efficient to intimate.

4

4 Windows not only let in natural light but are also an element of design. Here, the rectangular pattern of tile is mimicked in the small upper window tucked into the gable and in the mullions of the lower casement window.

5 Shaded by mini-blinds, this window glass wraps right around the corner, with no frame to interrupt the view.

5

ARTIFICIAL LIGHTING

1 Accent lighting concealed in the toe-kick area highlights the vanity while doing double-duty as an elegant nightlight. General lighting is supplied by a skylight and recessed-can fixtures overhead, while wall-mounted fixtures provide task lighting for the vanity area.

2 Known as a "suspended uplight," this Art Deco fixture directs incandescent light primarily toward the ceiling, turning it into a giant reflector that creates soft, shadowless general lighting in the room.

3 The most flattering vanity lighting, vertical cross-illumination, is provided by two fixtures placed at eye level on either side of the mirror. Here, two linear incandescent lights frame a stylish combination chrome-finished washbasin and attached mirror.

LIGHTING GUIDELINES
Light fixtures should be chosen to reflect the style of the bathroom and be placed to provide appropriate general and task lighting.

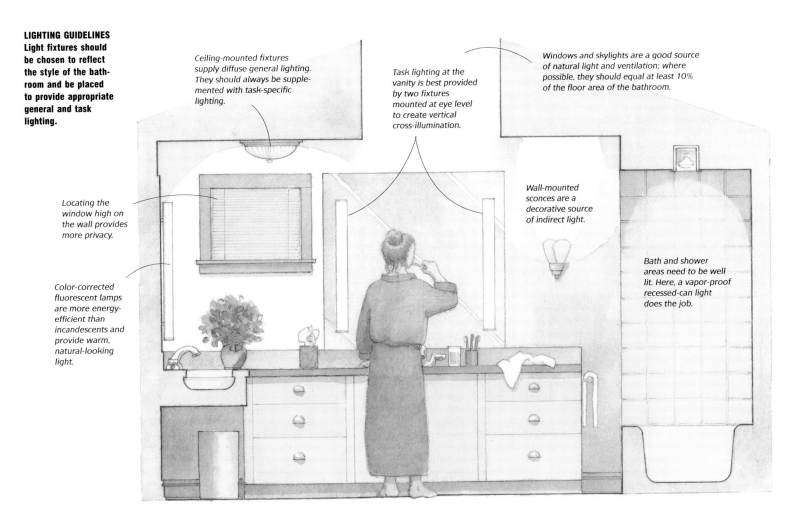

Ceiling-mounted fixtures supply diffuse general lighting. They should always be supplemented with task-specific lighting.

Task lighting at the vanity is best provided by two fixtures mounted at eye level to create vertical cross-illumination.

Windows and skylights are a good source of natural light and ventilation; where possible, they should equal at least 10% of the floor area of the bathroom.

Locating the window high on the wall provides more privacy.

Color-corrected fluorescent lamps are more energy-efficient than incandescents and provide warm, natural-looking light.

Wall-mounted sconces are a decorative source of indirect light.

Bath and shower areas need to be well lit. Here, a vapor-proof recessed-can light does the job.

DOING IT WITH MIRRORS

1 Plain round mirrors framed in pine reflect the simple design of this cottage bathroom.

2 An elaborately carved and gilded 18th-century French mirror adds a touch of opulence to the vanity area of this master bath. The gold-plated sink bowl and bronze-plated faucet are mounted on a marble countertop.

3 Even with the lights off, this bathroom has plenty of light, thanks to the mirrors that catch and reflect the daylight streaming in through the windows on the opposite wall.

4 Almost every surface—even a mirrored mini-blind—is a reflective one in this small bathroom. Diagonally laid tile and a "floating" vanity stretch the eye into the corners, making the 7-ft.-square bath feel larger than it is.

5 A simple oval wood-framed, beveledged mirror is warmly lit by a pair of wall-mounted fixtures fitted with incandescent lamps.

CLIMATE CONTROL

1 A radiant-heating system hidden beneath the marble tile is supplemented on cold Maine mornings by an electric heater mounted on the wall near the vanity. Concealed in the lighted teak valance above the sink is the air return for the heat-recovery ventilation system.

2 Simply opening this double-hung window provides natural ventilation. An electric towel-warming rack quickly dries wet towels and can supply a little bit of extra heat.

EVERYONE HAS A "COMFORT ZONE," and in the bathroom, where a lot of bare skin is exposed, it's about 5°F higher than in the rest of the house. Bathrooms should be warm enough to walk around in partially clothed or disrobed; a separate thermostat to control the bathroom's temperature is a good idea.

Ventilation needs to be reliable as well. Some windows and skylights are available with electric operators, so they can be opened or closed with the flick of a switch (convenient when a window is up out of reach). And if family members are forgetful about turning on the bath fan, try a humidity-sensing ventilation system that switches on automatically.

Double-hung

Slider

Awning

Transom (or hopper)

Casement

WINDOW STYLES
Different window styles offer different looks and should be chosen to match the house's architecture. Clad windows with wood cores offer the best combination of low maintenance, durability and resistance to rot, and insulative properties.

3 While bathroom ventilation is a practical necessity, this grille placed high in the gable wall conceals the fan and becomes an architectural element in the bathroom's design.

4 Two 250-watt infrared bulbs deliver instant, draft-free radiant warmth from a combination heater/ventilation fan. These lamps are more energy-efficient than blower-type units.

5 Warm-air registers are typically located near floor level to prevent air-stratification and drafts, but this ceiling-mounted grille has adjustable diffusers to control the volume and direction of warm air flowing into the room.

ALL ABOUT VENTILATION

A nice hot shower can raise a bathroom's humidity level to almost 100% in a matter of minutes. Though this humidity will slowly dissipate into the rest of the house after the shower is turned off, elevated humidity levels can cause all sorts of problems: peeling wallpaper, condensation on the windows, mildew, and mold. While an operable window can supply some bathrooms with all the ventilation they need, a fan is more reliable, easier to operate for children and the elderly, and more practical in cold weather.

Some bathroom fans seem as loud as helicopters (and are about as desirable to have operating in a small bathroom), but the new low-noise models are softer than a humming refrigerator in a quiet kitchen. Fan noise is measured in sones; steer clear of fans that have sone ratings higher than 3 because no one will want to switch them on. The best fans are rated at less than 1 sone and are barely audible when running. Some fans have humidistat controls that turn them on automatically when humidity levels are high.

Fans are sized according to the volume of air they can move in cubic feet per minute (cfm); the optimal air-change rate for residential bathrooms is about 8 air changes per hour. A quick formula for determining the size of fan you'll need is to multiply the floor area by 1.07 (assuming an 8-ft. ceiling). For example, a bathroom measuring 5 ft. by 9 ft. has 45 ft. of floor area; multiplied by 1.07, this equals 48.15. A bathroom this size would require a 50-cfm fan.

1 Strategically located beneath an elegantly simple towel bar constructed of common $1/2$-in. copper plumbing pipe, this electric towel warmer dries towels quickly and provides residual heat for the bathroom.

2 Available in either electric or hot-water configurations, wall-mounted panel radiators have variable heat outputs and can double as towel warmers.

3 Fin-tube hot-water baseboard radiation can prematurely rust from the moist environment encountered near a toilet. Lifting the radiator up away from floor level as shown here can help, though a better solution is to locate it on another wall.

4 Though the original steam-producing boilers that once powered them are, for the most part, long gone, old cast-iron radiators lend authentic charm to a period bath, as well as an impressive amount of heat.

If you can imagine an invisible and silent heating system that puts warmth exactly where you need it—at floor level—then you can imagine radiant heat. It is the perfect type of heat for a bathroom because it does away with clunky radiators, drafty and dusty air grilles, and baseboard fin-tube convectors that rust. Hidden in a floor, radiant heating offers even and predictable warmth that starts at your bare feet, whether the flooring is tile, wood, or carpet.

Radiant heat is surprisingly adaptable to both old and new bathrooms. It can be supplied either by hot water moving through tubes hidden in the floor (a hydronic system) or electrically, with cables, mats or electrical panels. Hydronic radiant heating is the most energy-efficient type of radiant heat, but new materials and techniques for installing electric radiant heat make this an appealing alternative.

If your home has a central hot-water heating system, it can probably be adapted to supply radiant heat. Special plastic tubing is installed under the finished floor (see the drawing at left) in a continuous loop, and hot water from the boiler circulates through it. While the materials and technology that have evolved over the last decade or so are new, the idea dates back to the Romans, and some of Frank Lloyd Wright's houses had radiantly heated floors.

Wright's radiant-heating systems consisted of copper pipes embedded in concrete slabs. But copper is expensive, tends to corrode and develop leaks in concrete, and is labor-intensive to install. Slab-type systems are still common, but now flexible plastic tubing is used. These slabs can be cast from concrete or from lighter-weight gypsum-based materials, making them adaptable to above-grade installations (for example, on a second floor). This flexible tubing can also be installed directly on or beneath a plywood subfloor, using aluminum heat-transfer plates to evenly distribute heat to the floor system. Hydronic radiant-heat systems have a long cycling time: They heat up and cool down slowly, so that the thermostat controlling them is typically left at a relatively constant setting and the rooms that are heated remain at a constant temperature.

Where a hydronic heat source isn't available, electric radiant heat can be a cost-effective alternative. Unlike hydronic radiant heat, most types of electric radiant heat have a quick response time. The heat can be turned on only when needed, like a light, and the room quickly warmed. After use, the system can be turned off again to conserve energy.

There are several different electrical radiant-heating methods. Perhaps the most versatile is a thin mat that is installed underneath tile. This system's main advantage is that it raises the finished floor elevation only about $1/8$ in. higher than it would normally be, making it a good choice for renovations. Besides tile, some types of hardwood flooring and carpeting can also be used with this system.

Another system relies on electrical cables that are installed either in a regular concrete slab or into the mortar bed into which tiles are set. A third type of system is a foil consisting of an electric heating element sandwiched between two layers of Mylar. Sheets of this foil can be installed beneath floors, behind walls, or in the ceiling.

A final type of radiant panel is comprised of a gypsum sheet embedded with electrical wiring. These $1/2$-in. panels can be installed and finished just like regular drywall, turning a wall or ceiling into a radiant surface. This type of system has a slower cycling time than other types of electric radiant heat.

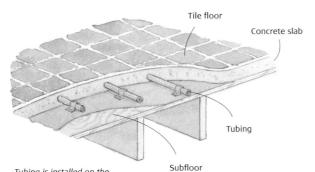

Tile floor
Concrete slab
Tubing
Subfloor

Tubing is installed on the subfloor and covered with cement. Tile is laid directly on the radiantly heated slab.

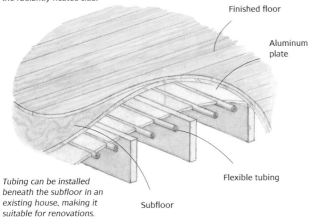

Finished floor
Aluminum plate
Flexible tubing
Subfloor

Tubing can be installed beneath the subfloor in an existing house, making it suitable for renovations.

5 There's nothing quite like a romantic soak in front of a fire. For practical reasons, this fire is fueled by natural gas, while the tile floor is warmed by an in-floor hydronic radiant-heating system.

RADIANT FLOOR HEATING In hydronic radiant-heating systems, hot water runs through a continuous loop of flexible plastic tubing hidden beneath the finished floor, carrying quiet and invisible warmth right where it is needed most: at floor level.

BEYOND THE
BASIC BATH

Think that acrylic whirlpools and electric steam generators are new ideas? Think again. While the technology may be new, the practice of immersing the body in heat, steam, or hot water is as old as civilization itself. The Japanese have onsen, or public mineral hot-spring baths. The hamman has long been a part of Islamic life. The Finns have their saunas, the Russians their banias, and Native Americans their sweat lodges.

Although the Romans didn't invent the idea of baths and bathing, they certainly elevated it to an art form. As early as the third century B.C., wealthy Romans were building elaborate personal bathing facilities in their villas and townhouses. These included rooms for both damp and dry heat, cold and warm tubs, and elaborate furnaces—called hypocausts—with flues extending through the floors and walls of the building to heat everything. Later they built public baths, including the smaller neighborhood *balneum* and larger, more elaborate *thermae*—that helped integrate bathing with everyday public life.

While the Romans may have gone overboard, they recognized and appreciated the restorative and healing properties of heat and hot water. With the notable exception of about a millennium's worth of western European civilization, most other cultures have too. There is an important message here that Americans are rediscovering and taking to heart: No need to make apologies about feeling good or to feel guilty about spending time attending to your own physical well-being, whether it is done communally or as a private affair. Water, in all of its forms, heals.

WINDOWS are kept clear of condensation by a sophisticated heat-recovery ventilation system. These windows look out over the Green Mountains of Vermont.

A LARGE WHIRLPOOL TUB can seat as many as six people. For many, a communal soak in hot water offers a chance to socialize with friends and family while revitalizing the body and nurturing the spirit.

HEAT is as elemental as water and can come from many different sources. Gentle radiant heat from this large room's in-floor radiant-heating system supplements the gas fireplace.

Saunas, Steamrooms, and Spas

1 While a prefabricated sauna (right) takes up a substantial amount of floor space, an acrylic steam shower (left) requires no more room than an ordinary combination tub/shower unit. A compact steam generator can often be added economically to an existing shower to give it steam capability.

2 The heat of a sauna, which can reach as high as 200°F, is great therapy for sore muscles. Regular practitioners swear by its ability to promote health and relaxation.

WATER IS ELEMENTAL, but the evolution of bathing facilities has long been linked with advances in technology. Modern manufacturing processes and modern materials like acrylic make it possible to economically produce our own private versions of once-public bathing facilities like the Roman *thermae*. Formerly found only in health clubs and expensive hotels, saunas and steamrooms have found their way into the home. For the cost of a steam generator or sauna heater, your spare closet or acrylic shower can become a haven from the stress of everyday life.

3 Sunken below the level of the radiantly heated tile floor, an organically shaped spa offers bathers a view of an outdoor zen garden through a nearby low window (not shown). Behind the glass door is a steam shower. The color scheme—stone, dark green, and deep blue—reflects colors found in nature.

1 A sophisticated heat-recovery ventilation system washes the many windows of this indoor spa with fresh air to prevent condensation, while an in-floor radiant-heating system keeps the marble-tile floor warm.

2 Made from a mixture of stone, copper, and glass, small mosaic tiles provide a shimmering surface for the sensuous curves of this spa.

SWEAT THERAPY

What's so hot about sweat? Well, for one thing, it's as essential as eating or breathing. Eliminate the body's ability to sweat by smothering the skin—think James Bond and Goldfinger—and it dies within hours. Sweat rids the body of waste and regulates its temperature, and it keeps the skin clean and elastic. The problem is, most of us don't sweat enough. Air-conditioning, antiperspirants, and inactivity all conspire to keep us sweat-free.

While saunas and steamshowers are relaxing, they also help the body to produce good clean sweat. During a 15-minute sauna, about a liter of sweat is excreted by the eccrine sweat glands that are located all over the body. This clear, odorless sweat un-clogs and cleanses skin pores and removes excessive salts, urea, and toxic heavy metals like copper, lead, mercury, and zinc. It also helps remove the lactic acid that is produced during exercise and that causes stiffness and fatigue.

Much like jogging or other forms of exercise, the heat of a steambath or sauna urges every organ of the body into action. Blood vessels dilate, the heart rate and metabolism increases, and the body's core temperature rises, making it difficult for some bacterial and viral agents to survive. Hard to believe that something that feels so good is so good for you.

3 Looking like a modern-day ruin, this indoor pool (right) was inspired by the Roman baths built two millennia ago. A loggia wraps around the pool, while a mahogany-floored rotunda connects the pool to the main house and provides space for a circular spa (far right).

4 A more intimately scaled whirlpool tub and accompanying footbath provides refuge from the pressures of the outside world. The phone is for outgoing calls only.

ALTERNATIVE SPACES

1 A simple outdoor shower transforms this garden space into a secluded oasis.

2 Marble and concrete help keep this Malibu beach house firmly grounded, while a soaring vaulted glass ceiling that extends across the entire house lifts the view upward toward the cliffs sheltering the beach.

THE IDEA OF SEGREGATING BATHING and personal hygiene into a separate closet-sized room has only been formalized in the last century. And while this may be an efficient use of space, efficiency is only one of several factors to be taken into account when designing a bathroom. New bathroom designs are more individualized, more responsive to site and climate, less constricted by architectural convention, and have a broader palette of materials to choose from.

The rediscovery of alternative spaces is a refreshing move away from conformity. If you live in a mild climate, why not have an outdoor shower? Why not put a shower stall or a soaking tub right in your bedroom? If there is enough room, why not include an exercise area, a small greenhouse, or a laundry area as part of the bathroom plan? And if you have a great view, why not take advantage of it?

3 Literally a water closet, a sand-blasted translucent-glass cubicle encloses the toilet in this otherwise open master bathroom.

JAPANESE BATHS

While Easterners' customs may sometimes seem inscrutable to Westerners, their bathing traditions make perfect sense for anyone who relishes a good soak. The Japanese have the good sense to view bathing as a ritual rather than a chore, a way to achieve spiritual contentment through the purification of the physical body. Whether done in private or (as is often the case) in one of the many public bathing facilities, personal cleanliness has long been an important aspect of Japanese culture.

Residential Japanese baths are small but deep, making them good for soaking but not so good for washing; washing and rinsing are done before you enter the bath. Usually, there will be a stool and a small bucket or basin nearby where you can sit, lather up, and then rinse off before slipping into the tub. After you're finished soaking, the tub remains filled for the next family member.

Public bath houses—or onsen—are located all over Japan and take advantage of the country's numerous mineral hot springs. Sometimes pool-like, sometimes indoors, and sometimes out, public baths usually have separate facilities for men and women. Again, showering, soaping, and rinsing are done before entering the bathing facilities; introducing soap bubbles into the baths is considered extremely bad etiquette, as is wearing clothing. After a serene and contemplative bath, many then take advantage of a shiatsu massage or relax with a beverage on tatami mats located nearby.

4 A Japanese-style soaking tub is ideal for those intent on total immersion in hot water. This short, deep, marble-tiled tub has removable teak duckboards on the interior for easy cleaning.

5 Aqua-green ceramic tile with the look of glass block separates the shower from the master bedroom. A pocket door slides out from the wall on the left when additional privacy is required.

6 French doors open wide to let in the mild California breezes and connect this swirling sunken spa with the garden.

1 A custom-fabricated stainless-steel tub stands in the middle of this spacious bathroom. Note the matching stainless-steel sink and doors leading to the toilet and shower on the far wall.

2 Designed for a couple with young children, this elegant bath features separate areas for the toilet, sinks, shower, and tub (defined by the columns), with entrances from both the hallway and the master bedroom.

WATER THERAPY

Most people are drawn to surf crashing on an ocean beach. The sound is overpowering, the motion of the waves almost hypnotic; you come away feeling awed and revitalized. The secret? Not the sun, the water, or the wind, but negative ions.

Ionization occurs when enough energy—water crashing on a beach, water splashed on the hot rocks of a sauna—acts on a molecule to cause it to lose an electron. While the old molecule becomes positively charged, the lost, negatively charged electron soon attaches itself to another molecule, causing it to become negatively charged itself: a negative ion. Medical researchers consider these negative ions, which can also be caused by cosmic rays, radiation, and photosynthesis, to be beneficial, while too many positive ions result in fatigue and anxiety and have been linked to heart attacks, allergies, insomnia, and arthritis.

Negative ions can be produced by simple negative-ion generators (a technology commonly used in hospitals and businesses with closed-circuit air systems) or by splashing water on hot rocks heated by a woodburning sauna stove to create steam—it isn't nearly as practical, but it's a lot more fun.

While you're charging your ions with hot water, charge your body with cold water. Though some hardy souls start the day with a cold shower, it's easier to end a hot bath or steamy sauna with a cold dip. The Romans jumped into a pool full of cold water; the Finns jump into the snow. Either way, the cold closes the pores and stimulates the body, leaving you clean, relaxed, and alert.

3 An antique chandelier overhead, a patterned marble floor underneath, and curved walls all around focus attention on the whirlpool tub. The custom-built vanity tucked into the alcove has concave mirrored-glass drawer fronts, while large double doors lead to the master bedroom.

1 The canopy bath-tub was moved out of a corner and into the center of the room during an extensive remodel. It features a hand-painted scene depicting the front of the house overlooking a small lake; the cat belongs to the family. The fireplace (right) was once located in a separate sitting area; removing a partition wall made this bath-room larger and more luxurious and made room for an additional sink.

2 A highly polished stone-slab shelf reflects the view through a large window to the hillside beyond, echoing the calm, mirrorlike quality of the water in the tub.

3 The next best thing to standing under a natural waterfall is this custom body-spa—or does the warm water make it even better?

4 Pampered from head to toe: a recirculating bubble footbath, hydromassage body jets from knee to shoulder level, and a cascading waterfall shower. You'll never want to leave.

CONSIDER THE OLD RULES of bathroom design broken. Feel free to combine old materials with new, old fixtures with new. Or look for the newest, the latest and greatest on the Internet. Choose what you like for many different reasons—for looks, for features, for durability, for nostalgia—but, most important, because they make you feel good.

As the hundreds of bathrooms featured in this book clearly show, a bathroom is a highly personal and individualized space. There's a whole world out there for inspiration and ideas, and no right or wrong approaches. Isn't it about time to start transforming your own bathroom into the space you want it to be?

With the advent of the Internet, information about bathrooms—about design and construction, about manufacturers and their products, about different materials—is often but a few keystrokes away. But the vast amount of information available on the Internet doesn't have much shape or structure; for that, turn to some of the magazines, books, and associations listed here.

Here, too, you'll find a list of manufacturers that assisted in producing this book; they (and other manufacturers) can be contacted for catalogs and specific information about their products.

MAGAZINES

American Homestyle & Gardening
375 Lexington Avenue
New York, NY 10017–5514
www.dreamremodeling.com

Fine Homebuilding
The Taunton Press
63 South Main Street
Newtown, CT 06470
www.taunton.com

Kitchen and Bath Business
One Penn Plaza, 10th Floor
New York, NY 10119
www.kitchen-bath.com

Kitchen and Bath Design News
445 Broad Hollow Road
Melville, NY 11747
www.kitchenandbathexpo.com

BOOKS

Calloway, Stephen and Elizabeth Cromley (Eds.). *The Elements of Style.* New York: Simon & Schuster, 1996.
An excellent graphic overview of the visual elements that make up the specific styles that have influenced British and American architecture over the last 500 years.

Cheever, Ellen. *The Basics of Bathroom Design...and Beyond.* Hackettstown, NJ: National Kitchen and Bath Association (NKBA), 1989.
Intended for industry professionals, a comprehensive survey of materials and fixture types, with planning and design guidelines and floor plans and elevations of specific types of bathrooms.

National Kitchen and Bath Association. *The Essential Bathroom Design Guide.* New York: John Wiley & Sons, 1997.
Based on the NKBA's six-volume manual for their training program for bathroom designers, this book offers technical guidance on bathroom planning and design, as well as the best presentation and explanation of NKBA's *41 Guidelines of Bathroom Planning* that I've seen.

Peterson, Mary Jo. *Universal Kitchen and Bathroom Planning: Designs that Adapt to People.* New York: McGraw-Hill, 1997.
Thorough and practical information about how to design kitchens and baths that suit the needs of all users throughout their lives.

Sacks, Diane Dorrans. *Bathrooms.* San Francisco, CA: Chronicle Books, 1998.
While the focus is definitely on California, this is probably the best of the many books on bathroom style.

Wormer, Andrew. *The Builder's Book of Bathrooms.* Newtown, CT: The Taunton Press, 1998.
A practical planning and construction guide intended primarily for builders, this book offers design information useful to homeowners who are interested in the nuts and bolts of how a bathroom goes togther.

Wylde, Margaret, Adrian Baron-Robbins and Sam Clark. *Building for a Lifetime: The Design and Construction of Fully Accessible Homes.* Newtown, CT: The Taunton Press, 1994.
A complete and readable guide for designers, builders, and homeowners to accessible design in interior and exterior spaces.

ASSOCIATIONS AND AGENCIES

American Lighting Association
World Trade Center, Suite 10046
P.O. Box 420288
Dallas, TX 75342-0288
(800) 605-4448
www.americanlightingassoc.com

Home Ventilating Institute
30 West University Drive
Arlington Heights, IL 60004-1893
(847) 394-0150

Kitchen Cabinets Manufacturers Association (KCMA)
1899 Preston White Drive
Reston, VA 20191-5435
(703) 264-1690
www.kcma.org

Marble Institute of America
30 Eden Alley, Suite 301
Columbus, OH 43215
(614) 228-6194
www.marble-institute.com

National Kitchen and Bath Association (NKBA)
687 Willow Grove St.
Hackettstown, NJ 07840
(800) 843-6522
www.nkba.org
www.kitchenet.com

Porcelain Enamel Institute
P.O. Box 158541
4004 Hillsboro Pike, Suite 224B
Nashville, TN 37215
(615) 385-5357
http://porcelainenamel.org

Tile Council of America (TCA)
100 Clemson Research Blvd.
Anderson, SC 29625
(864) 646-8453
www.tileusa.com

MANUFACTURERS

The following manufacturers contributed valuable advice and photography to this book. Most manufacturers maintain useful websites offering product information, technical support, new products, and dealer information. They can usually be accessed on the Internet simply by trying www."companyname".com (e.g., www.alsons.com) or by using your favorite search engine.

Absolute by American Standard
6615 West Boston Street
Chandler, AZ 85226
(800) 359-3261
European luxury bath suites complete with sinks, toilets, bidets, and tubs.

Advanced Ventilation Technologies
P.O. Box 2269
Chino Valley, AZ 86323
(888) 552-3836
Automatic toilet and room exhaust systems.

Alsons Corporation
42 Union Street
Hillsdale, MI 49242
(517) 439-1411
Handshowers, showerheads, adjustable tracks, and accessories.

American Chinaware
6615 West Boston Street
Chandler, AZ 85226
(800) 359-3261
Complete bath suites in standard and custom hand-painted designs and colors.

American Standard
One Centennial Avenue
P.O. Box 6820
Piscataway, NJ 08855-6320
(908) 980-3132
Residential bathroom fixtures and faucets.

Aqua Glass Corporation
P.O. Box 412
Industrial Park
Adamsville, TN 38310
(800) 238-3940
Tubs, whirlpools, and showers featuring Microban antibacterial protection.

Barclay Products Limited
4000 Porett Drive
Gurnee, IL 60031
(847) 244-1234
Traditional and contemporary bath fixtures and accessories.

Bisazza North America
8530 Northwest 30th Terrace
Miami, FL 33122
(305) 597-4099
Glass mosaic tiles.

Briggs Industries, Inc.
4350 West Cypress Street, Suite 800
Tampa, FL 33607
(813) 878-0178
Residential, commercial, and ADA-compliant toilets.

Broan
926 West State Street
Hartford, WI 53027
(800) 445-6057
Ventilation, lighting, and bathroom storage products.

Delta Faucet
A Division of Masco Corp. of Indiana
55 East 111th Street
P.O. Box 40980
Indianapolis, IN 46280
(800) 345-3358
Tub, sink, and shower faucets.

Diamond Spas, Inc.
760 South 104th Street
Broomfield, CO 80020
(800) 951-7727
Stainless-steel sinks, spas and tubs.

Eljer
17120 Dallas Parkway
Dallas, TX 75248
(214) 407-2600
Bath fixtures and faucets.

Feeny Manufacturing Co.
P.O. Box 191
Muncie, IN 47308
(800) 899-6535
Bath storage and organization accessories.

Finnleo Saunas, Inc.
575 East Cokato Street
Cokato, MN 55321
(800) 346-6536
Sauna kits, heaters, and accessories

Formica Corporation
10155 Reading Rd.
Cincinnati, OH 45241-4805
(800) 367-6422
Plastic, wood, and metal laminates and solid-surfacing products.

Geberit Manufacturing, Inc.
1100 Boone Drive
Michigan City, IN 46360
(219) 879-4466
Innovative toilets and bathroom accessories.

Gerber Plumbing Fixtures Corp.
4600 Touhy Avenue
Chicago, IL 60646
(847) 675-6570
Faucets and vitreous china fixtures.

Grohe
241 Covington Dr.
Bloomingdale, IL 60108
(630) 582-7711
Bathroom sink, tub, and shower faucets.

HEWI, Inc.
2851 Old Tree Drive
Lancaster, PA 17603
(717) 293-1313
Universal bathroom design products.

Image/PS Craftsmanship
10-40 Jackson Avenue
Long Island City, NY 11101
(718) 729-3686
Sculptural wood sinks, tubs, and vanity tops.

Jacuzzi
2121 North California Boulevard,
Suite 475
Walnut Creek, CA 94596
(800) 678-6889
Whirlpool industry pioneer offering tubs, shower systems, and faucets.

Kohler
444 Highland Drive
Kohler, WI 53044
(920) 457-4441
Bathroom fixtures and accessories, including tubs, faucets, and sinks.

Lasco Bathware, Inc.
3255 East Miraloma Avenue
Anaheim, CA 92806
(800) 877-0464
Acrylic showers, tubs, and whirlpools.

Maax
600 Cameron
Sainte-Marie, Beauce
Quebec, Canada G6E 1B2
(418) 387-4155
Acrylic, fiberglass, and ABS tubs, whirlpools, showers, and shower doors.

Moen
P.O. Box 8022
North Olmsted, OH 44070-8022
(216) 962-2000
Tub, sink, and shower faucets.

Myson, Inc.
49 Hercules Drive
Colchester, VT 05446
(800) 698-9690
Electric and hydronic towel warmers and heaters.

Otto Bock Reha
3000 Xenium Lane, North
Minneapolis, MN 55441
(800) 328-4058
Universal bathroom design products.

Panasonic
One Panasonic Way—4A-5
Secaucus, NJ 07094
(201) 271-3287
Ventilating fans and Intimist toilet seat.

Porcher
6615 West Boston Street
Chandler, AZ 85226
(800) 359-3261
Luxury imported bath fixtures, with styles ranging from turn-of-the-century to Euro-contemporary.

Runtal North America
187 Neck Road
P.O. Box 8278
Ward Hill, MA 01835
(800) 526-2621
Euro-style radiators and towel warmers.

Toto
1155 Southern Road
Morrow, GA 30260
(800) 938-1541
World's largest plumbing manufacturer, featuring innovative toilets and accessories.

Wilsonart International
2400 Wilson Place
P.O. Box 6110
Temple, TX 76503-6110
(800) 433-3222
Plastic laminate and solid-surface products.

GREAT BATHROOM DESIGNS

pp. 6-7 DESIGN: Sharon Hopkins; PHOTO: David Duncan Livingston, NKBA

pp. 8-9 #1 DESIGN: Sandra L. Steiner-Houck/Marianne Heidelbaugh, Mechanicsburg, PA; PHOTO: Peter Margonelli, NKBA; #2 DESIGN: Lynn David Monson/Monson Interior Design; PHOTO: Nancy Hill, NKBA; #3 DESIGN: William McClay Architects & Planners, AIA, Warren, VT; PHOTO: Carolyn L. Bates; #4 DESIGN: Tom Cabot, Shelburne, VT; PHOTOS: Carolyn L. Bates

pp. 10-11 #1 PHOTO: Grey Crawford; #2 PHOTO: Brian Vanden Brink; #3 PHOTO: Eric Roth #4 DESIGN: Peter Feinmann, Arlington, MA; PHOTO: Steve Vierra; #5 DESIGN: Brad Rabinowitz, Burlington, VT; PHOTO: Carolyn L. Bates; #6 DESIGN: Patricia El-Baz, Concord, MA; PHOTO: Eric Roth

pp. 12-13 #1 DESIGN: Gary White, CID, CKD, CBD, Kitchen & Bath Design, Newport Beach, CA; PHOTO: Larry Falke; #2 DESIGN: Sam Scofield, AIA, Stowe, VT; PHOTO: Carolyn L. Bates; #3 DESIGN: Delores Hyden, CKD, CBD, Showplace Design & Remodeling, Redmond, WA; PHOTO: Roger Turk/Northlight Photography; #4 DESIGN: Stephen R. Tobin; PHOTO: Kevin Ireton/*Fine Homebuilding* magazine, ©The Taunton Press; #5 DESIGN: Klaudia Norlen, Denver, CO; PHOTO: David Duncan Livingston

pp. 14-15 #1 DESIGN: Brad Rabinowitz, Burlington, VT; PHOTO: Carolyn L. Bates; #2 DESIGN: Susan Larsen, PHOTO: Michael Skott, NKBA; #3 DESIGN: Jere Bowden, CKD, Rutt of Atlanta, Atlanta, GA; PHOTO: John Umberger #4 DESIGN: Kathie Wheaton; PHOTOS: Roe Osborne/*Fine Homebuilding* magazine, ©The Taunton Press

pp. 16-17 #1 DESIGN: Showplace Design & Remodeling, Redmond, WA; PHOTO: David Duncan Livingston; #2 DESIGN: Dena Jurries, Treasure Valley Woodworking, Nampa, ID; PHOTO: David Duncan Livingston; #3 DESIGN: Jeff Hill/Hill Custom Homes; PHOTO: Roger Turk/Northlight Photography; #4 DESIGN: Ironies, Oakland, CA; PHOTO: David Duncan Livingston; #5 DESIGN: Acorn Kitchens & Baths, Oakland, CA; PHOTO: David Duncan Livingston

pp. 18-19 #1 DESIGN: Van Martin Rowe; PHOTO: Jeremy Samuelson; #2 DESIGN: Jere Bowden, CKD, Rutt of Atlanta, Atlanta, GA; PHOTO: John Umberger; #3 DESIGN: Gary White, CID, CKD, CBD, Kitchen & Bath Design, Newport Beach, CA; PHOTO: Larry Falke; #4 PHOTO: Courtesy HEWI, Inc.; #5 DESIGN: The Snyder Companies; PHOTO: Carolyn L. Bates

pp. 20-21 #1 DESIGN: Suzanne Tucker, Tucker & Marks, San Francisco, CA; PHOTO: Tim Street-Porter; #2 DESIGN: Leanne Croft Interiors, Andover, MA; PHOTO: Steve Vierra; #3 DESIGN: Phillip Jude Miller/American Dural, Cambridge, MA; PHOTO: Eric Roth; #4 DESIGN: Miller/Dolezal, Woodside, CA PHOTO: David Duncan Livingston; #5 DESIGN: Kay McKallagat, Kay Bailey McKallagat Interior Design, West Newbury, MA; PHOTO: Steve Vierra

pp. 22-23 #1 PHOTO: Jeremy Samuelson; #2 DESIGN: Martin Van Rowe; PHOTO: Jeremy Samuelson; #3 PHOTO: courtesy HEWI, Inc.

pp. 24-25 #1 PHOTO: Brian Vanden Brink; #2 DESIGN: Greg Rawson, Richards Kitchen & Bath Center, Muncie, IN; PHOTO: David Duncan Livingston; #3 DESIGN: Classic Post & Beam; PHOTO: Brian Vanden Brink; #4 DESIGN: Miller/Stein, Menlo Park, CA; PHOTO: David Duncan Livingston; #5 PHOTO: courtesy Porcher

pp. 26-27 #1 DESIGN: Nancy Scheinholtz, San Francisco, CA; PHOTO: David Duncan Livingston; #2 DESIGN: Lenny Steinberg, Lenny Steinberg Design Assoc.,Venice, CA; PHOTO: Tim Street-Porter; #3 DESIGN: Janet Moody; PHOTO: Scott Gibson, *Fine Homebuilding* magazine, ©The Taunton Press; #4 DESIGN: Osburn Design, San Francisco,CA; PHOTO: David Duncan Livingston

pp. 28-29 #1 DESIGN: Steven Magliocco Associates, Boston, MA; INTERIOR DESIGN: Nancy Eddy Inc., Dedham, MA; CABINETRY: George Verry, Pembroke, MA; PHOTO: Steve Vierra; #2 PHOTO: David Duncan Livingston; #3 DESIGN: Carleen Cafferty Interior Design, NWSID; PHOTO: Roger Turk; #4 PHOTO: David Duncan Livingston; #5 DESIGN: Tom Cabot, Shelburne, VT; PHOTO: Carolyn L. Bates

pp. 30-31 #1 DESIGN: Tony Simmonds; PHOTOS: Charles Miller/*Fine Homebuilding* magazine, ©The Taunton Press; #2 PHOTO: Grey Crawford; #3 DESIGN: Steven M. Levine/Lonnie Weinstein, Euro-Plus Design, Inc., Needham, MA; PHOTO: Andrew Bordwin, NKBA; #4 DESIGN: Steve Jacobson/Siri Evju; PHOTO: Stephen Cridland, NKBA

pp. 32-33 #1 DESIGN: Mary Jo Peterson, Brookfield, CT; PHOTOS: William Lebovich; #2 PHOTO: courtesy, HEWI, Inc.; #3 PHOTO: courtesy Otto Bock Reha

FINISHING THE BATH IN STYLE

pp. 34-35 DESIGN: Peter Feinmann, Arlington, MA; PHOTO: Steve Vierra

pp. 36-37 #1 DESIGN: Ruth Reynar/Artistic Dimensions, West Barnstable, MA; PHOTO: Steve Vierra; #2 DESIGN: Sharon Alber Fannin/Fannin Interiors, Inc., Paradise Valley, AZ; PHOTO: David Duncan Livingston; #3 DESIGN: Scott Cornelius/Scott Cornelius Architects, NY, NY; PHOTO: Carolyn L. Bates; #4 DESIGN: Scott Cornelius/Scott Cornelius Architects, NY, NY; PHOTO: Carolyn L. Bates;

#5 DESIGN: Victoria Holland, Bellevue, WA; PHOTO: Andrew Wormer/*Fine Homebuilding* magazine, ©The Taunton Press

pp. 38-39 #1 DESIGN: Curtis Gelotte Architects, Kirkland, WA; PHOTO: Roger Turk/Northlight Photography; #2 PHOTO: David Duncan Livingston; #3 DESIGN: Sandra Vitzthum Architect, Montpelier, VT; PHOTO: Carolyn L. Bates; #4 PHOTO: David Duncan Livingston; #5 DESIGN: Carlton Winslow; CONSTRUCTION: Joe Campanelli; PHOTO: Steve Culpepper/*Fine Homebuilding* magazine, ©The Taunton Press

pp. 40-41 #1 DESIGN: Peachtree Designs; PHOTO: Steve Vierra; #2 DESIGN: Donna Ridell, Victoria, BC Canada; PHOTO: David Duncan Livingston; #3 DESIGN: Agnes Bourne, San Francisco, CA; PHOTO: David Duncan Livingston; #4 DESIGN: Suzanne Tucker, Tucker & Marks, San Francisco, CA; PHOTO: Tim Street-Porter; #5 DESIGN: Arthur Krikor Halajian/ Kitchens & More, San Rafael, CA; PHOTO: David Duncan Livingston

pp. 42-43 #1 PHOTO: Jeremy Samuelson; #2 DESIGN: Beverly Rivkind & Lisa Lipschutz, Beverly Rivkind Interior Design, Norwell, MA; PHOTO: Steve Vierra; #3 DESIGN: Gary White CID, CKD, CBD, Kitchen & Bath Design, Newport Beach, CA; PHOTO: Larry Falke; #4 CONSTRUCTION: John Campbell; PHOTO: Carolyn L. Bates

pp. 44-45 #1 DESIGN: Carolyn Schmitz, Newport, RI; PHOTO: Steve Vierra; #2 PHOTO: David Duncan Livingston; #3 DESIGN: Suzanne Tucker, Tucker & Marks, San Francisco, CA; PHOTO: Tim Street Porter; #4 DESIGN: Marie Thompson, Showplace Design & Remodeling, Redmond, WA; PHOTOS: Roger Turk/Northlight Photography

pp. 46-47 #1 DESIGN: David Hodge; PHOTO: Charles Miller/*Fine Homebuilding* magazine, ©The Taunton Press; #2 PHOTO: ©PhotoPic/Camerique; #3 DESIGN: Brad Rabinowitz, Burlington, VT; PHOTO: Carolyn L. Bates

pp. 48-49 #1 DESIGN: Victoria Holland; PHOTO: Andrew Wormer/*Fine Homebuilding* magazine, ©The Taunton Press; #2 DESIGN: Brad Rabinowitz, Burlington, VT; PHOTO: Carolyn L. Bates; #3 DESIGN: Donna Christopher; PHOTO: Carolyn L. Bates; #4 DESIGN: Werner Design Associates; PHOTO: David Duncan Livingston; #5 PHOTO: David Duncan Livingston

pp. 50-51 #1 DESIGN: Jeffrey Tohl, The Architecture Studio, Inc., Los Angeles, CA; PHOTO: Tim Street-Porter; #2 DESIGN: Brian A. Murphy, BAM Construction/Design, Inc., Santa Monica, CA; PHOTO: Tim Street-Porter; #3 DESIGN: Brian A.Murphy, BAM Construction/Design, Inc., Santa Monica, CA; PHOTO: Tim Street-Porter; #4 DESIGN: Robert Blanchard; TILE: Lisa Winkler, Burlington, VT; PHOTO: Carolyn L. Bates; #5 DESIGN: MB Cushman Design, Inc., Stowe, VT; TILE: Michael Byrne; PHOTO: Carolyn L. Bates

pp. 52-53 **#1** PHOTO: David Duncan Livingston **#2** DESIGN: James Vivrette, Altera Design & Remodeling, Orinda, CA; PHOTO: David Duncan Livinston, NKBA; **#3** DESIGN: Fu-Tung Cheng, Berkeley, CA; PHOTO: David Duncan Livinston; **#4** DESIGN: GKW Working Design, Stowe, VT; PHOTO: Carolyn L. Bates; **#5** DESIGN: Lee Moller PHOTO: Jefferson Kolle/ *Fine Homebuilding* magazine, ©The Taunton Press

pp. 54-55 **#1** DESIGN: Kelly Davis; PHOTO: *Fine Homebuilding* magazine, ©The Taunton Press; **#2** DESIGN: Carney Architects, Jackson, WY; PHOTO: Charles Miller/*Fine Homebuilding* magazine, ©The Taunton Press; **#3** DESIGN: Sam Scofield, AIA, Stowe, VT; PHOTO: Carolyn L. Bates; **#4** DESIGN: Erica Westeroth, XTC Design, Inc.; PHOTO: Virginia McDonald, NKBA; **#5** DESIGN:Julie Erreca and Pierre Bourriague, Felton, CA; PHOTO: Charles Miller/*Fine Homebuilding* magazine, ©The Taunton Press; **#6** DESIGN: Joszi Meskan Associates, San Francisco, CA; FLOOR: Willem Racké; PHOTO: David Duncan Livingston

pp. 56-57 **#1** DESIGN: Tom Edwards; GLASS: Tom Horton, Sandman Art Glass, Wallingford, CT; PHOTOS: Charles Miller/*Fine Homebuilding* magazine, ©The Taunton Press; **#2** DESIGN: Ron Braun; TUB: David Hertz; PHOTO: Jeremy Samuelson; **#3** DESIGN: Jack Wilbern; PHOTO: Scott Gibson/*Fine Homebuilding* magazine, ©The Taunton Press; **#4** DESIGN: Charles and Lucy Metcalf; PHOTO: Charles Miller/*Fine Homebuilding* magazine, ©The Taunton Press

pp. 58-59 **#1** PHOTO: Grey Crawford; **#2** DESIGN: Brian Brand; PHOTO: Charles Miller/*Fine Homebuilding* magazine, ©The Taunton Press; **#3** DESIGN: Molly Korb CKD, CBD/MK Designs, Newcastle, CA; PHOTOS: David Duncan Livingston; **#4** PHOTO: Grey Crawford

pp. 60-61 **#1** DESIGN: Classic Post & Beam; PHOTO: Brian Vanden Brink; **#2** DESIGN: Steven Levine/Lonnie Weinstein, Euro-Plus Design, Inc., Needham, MA; PHOTO: Andrew Brodwin, NKBA; **#3** DESIGN: Lee Moller; PHOTO: Jefferson Kolle/ *Fine Homebuilding* magazine, ©The Taunton Press; **#4** DESIGN: Steven Strong, Solar Design Associates, Harvard, MA; PHOTO: Brian Vanden Brink

pp. 62-63 **#1** DESIGN: Michelle Rolens, Neil Kelly Designers/Remodelers, Portland, OR; PHOTO: Nick Garibo, NKBA; **#2 (top, middle)** DESIGN: Greg Rawson, Richards Kitchen & Bath Center, Muncie, IN; PHOTO: David Duncan Livingston; **#2 (bottom)** PHOTO: David Duncan Livingston; **#3** PHOTO: David Duncan Livingston; **#4** DESIGN: Delores Hyden CKD, CBD, Showplace Design & Remodeling, Redmond, WA; PHOTO: Roger Turk/Northlight Photography

pp. 64-65 **#1** PHOTO: courtesy Formica; **#2** DESIGN: Greg Rawson, Richards Kitchen & Bath Center, Muncie, IN; PHOTO: David Duncan Livingston; **#3** PHOTO: courtesy Formica; **#4** DESIGN: Delores Hyden CKD, CBD, Showplace Design & Remodeling, Redmond, WA; PHOTO: Roger Turk/Northlight Photography; **#5** PHOTO: courtesy Formica

pp. 66-67 **#1** DESIGN: Armando Ruiz y Perez, Armando Ruiz Diseno SA, Mexico; TROMPE L'OEIL: Jill Beardsley; PHOTO: David Duncan Livingston; **#2** DESIGN: Sharon Campbell Interior Design, San Anselmo, CA; PHOTO: David Duncan Livingston; **#3** DESIGN: Julie Atwood, Petaluma, CA; PHOTO: David Duncan Livingston; **#4** DESIGN: Vivienne Weil/Decorative Interiors, Inc., Manchester, VT; PHOTO: Steve Vierra

BATHTUBS
& SHOWERS

pp. 68-69 DESIGN: Pierre Koenig, Los Angeles, CA; PHOTO: Tim Street-Porter

pp. 70-71 **#1** DESIGN: Karin Thomas Interior Designs; PHOTO: Brian Vanden Brink; **#2** DESIGN: Delores Hyden, CKD, CBD, Showplace Design & Remodeling, Redmond, WA; PHOTO: David Duncan Livingston; **#3** PHOTO: Brian Vanden Brink; **#4** PHOTO: Brian Vanden Brink; **#5** PHOTO: Grey Crawford

pp. 72-73 **#1** DESIGN: Van Martin Rowe; PHOTO: Tim Street-Porter; **#2** PHOTO: Tim Street Porter; **#3** DESIGN: Ray Kappe; PHOTO: Brian Vanden Brink; **#4** PHOTO: David Duncan Livingston; **#5** PHOTO: Jeremy Samuelson; **#6** PHOTO: David Duncan Livingston; **#7** PHOTO: Carolyn L. Bates

pp. 74-75 **#1** DESIGN: Sandra Steiner-Houck, CKD/Marianne Heidelbaugh; PHOTO: Peter Margonelli, NKBA; **#2** DESIGN: Charles Rand; PHOTO: Charles Miller/*Fine Homebuilding* magazine, ©The Taunton Press; **#3** DESIGN: Acorn Kitchen & Bath, Oakland, CA; PHOTO: David Duncan Livingston; **#4** PHOTO: Eric Roth

pp. 76-77 **#1** PHOTO: Brian Vanden Brink; **#2** DESIGN: Brian A. Murphy, BAM Construction/Design, Inc., Santa Monica, CA; PHOTO: Tim Street-Porter; **#3** DESIGN: Michael Dugan, AIA; PHOTO: Carolyn L. Bates; **#4** DESIGN: J. Graham Goldsmith Architects, Burlington, VT; PHOTO: Carolyn L. Bates

pp. 78-79 **#1** PHOTO: courtesy Kohler; **#2** PHOTO: courtesy Jacuzzi; **#3** PHOTO: courtesy Maax; **#4** PHOTO: courtesy Aquaglass

pp. 80-81 **#1** DESIGN: Steve Taylor; PHOTO: Bruce Greenlaw/*Fine Homebuilding* magazine, ©The Taunton Press; **#2** PHOTO: courtesy Aquaglass; **#3** PHOTOS: courtesy Kohler; **#4** PHOTO: courtesy Jacuzzi; **#5** PHOTO: courtesy Maax

pp. 82-83 **#1** PHOTO: David Duncan Livingston; **#2** DESIGN: Judith Bracht/Richard M. Tunis Inc.; PHOTO: Peter Margonelli, NKBA; **#3** DESIGN: Ken Payson; PHOTO: Tim Street-Porter; **#4** DESIGN: Mark Mack; PHOTO: Tim Street-Porter; **#5** DESIGN: Margie Little, CKD,CBD; PHOTO: David Duncan Livingston

pp. 84-85 **#1** DESIGN: Brian A. Murphy, BAM Construction/Design, Inc., Santa Monica, CA; PHOTO: Tim Street-Porter; **#2** DESIGN: M.B. Cushman Design Inc., Stowe, VT; PHOTO: Carolyn L. Bates; **#3** PHOTO: courtesy Grohe; **#4** PHOTO: courtesy Jacuzzi; **#5** DESIGN: David Hall,The Henry Klein Partnership Architects, Mt Vernon, WA; PHOTO: David Hall; **#6** PHOTO: courtesy Kohler; **#7** DESIGN: Brian A. Murphy, BAM Construction/Design, Inc., Santa Monica, CA; PHOTO: Tim Street-Porter

pp. 86-87 **#1** DESIGN: M.B. Cushman Design Inc., Stowe, VT; PHOTO: Carolyn L. Bates; **#2** DESIGN: Karen Richmond, Neil Kelly Designers/ Remodelers, Portland, OR; PHOTO: David Duncan Livingston; **#3** DESIGN: Brad Rabinowitz, Burlington, VT; PHOTO: Carolyn L. Bates; **#4** PHOTO: courtesy Kohler; **#5** DESIGN: Greg Richard Rawson, CKD, CBD/Richard's Kitchen & Bath Center; PHOTO: Andrew Bordwin, NKBA

pp. 88-89 **#1** DESIGN: Brad Rabinowitz, Burlington, VT; PHOTO: Carolyn L. Bates; **#2** DESIGN: Brad Rabinowitz, Burlington, VT; PHOTO: Carolyn L. Bates; **#3** DESIGN: Suzanne Tucker, Tucker & Marks, San Francisco, CA; PHOTO: Tim Street-Porter; **#4** DESIGN: Steven M. Foote, FAIA, Perry Dean Rogers & Partners, Boston, MA; PHOTO: Brian Vanden Brink; **#5** PHOTO: courtesy Absolute by American Standard; **#6** DESIGN: Karen Richmond, Neil Kelly Designers/Remodelers, Portland, OR; PHOTO: David Duncan Livingston; **#7** PHOTO: courtesy Absolute by American Standard

TOILETS
& SINKS

pp. 90-91 PHOTO: courtesy Absolute by American Standard

pp. 92-93 **#1** PHOTO: Carolyn L. Bates; **#2** PHOTO: courtesy Barclay Products Ltd.; **#3** DESIGN: Kitchens & More, San Rafael, CA; PHOTO: David Duncan Livingston, NKBA; **#4** PHOTO: courtesy Absolute by American Standard

pp. 94-95 **#1** PHOTO: courtesy Eljer; **#2** DESIGN: Lynn Williams Interiors; PHOTO: Carolyn L. Bates; **#3** DESIGN: M.B. Cushman Design Inc., Stowe, VT; PHOTO: Carolyn L. Bates; **#4** PHOTO: courtesy Briggs Industries, Tampa, FL; **#5** PHOTO: courtesy Kohler; **#6** DESIGN: Paul Wiseman; PHOTO: David Duncan Livingston

pp. 96-97 **#1** PHOTO: courtesy Toto; **#2** DESIGN: Ruth Reynar/Artistic Dimensions; PHOTO: Steve Vierra; **#3** PHOTO: courtesy Panasonic; **#4** DESIGN: M.B. Cushman Design Inc., Stowe, VT; PHOTO: Carolyn L. Bates; **#5** PHOTO: courtesy Kohler; **#6** PHOTO: courtesy Kohler

pp. 98-99 **#1** DESIGN: Agnes Bourne, San Francisco, CA; PHOTO: David Duncan Livingston; **#2** PHOTO: courtesy Absolute by American Standard; **#3** PHOTO: courtesy Advanced Ventilation Technologies; **#4** PHOTO: courtesy Toto; **#5** PHOTO: courtesy Toto; **#6** DESIGN: Richards Kitchen & Bath Center, Muncie, IN; PHOTO: David Duncan Livingston

pp. 100-101 **#1** PHOTO: courtesy Absolute by American Standard; **#2** PHOTO: courtesy Porcher; **#3** DESIGN: Ted Montgomery/Indiana Architecture & Design, Charlotte, VT; PHOTO: Carolyn L. Bates; **#4** PHOTO: courtesy Kohler; **#5** PHOTO: courtesy Kohler; **#6** DESIGN: Michael Dugan, AIA, Essex, VT; PHOTO: Carolyn L. Bates

pp. 102-103 **#1** PHOTO: Carolyn L. Bates; **#2** DESIGN: Donna Koziol Interior Design, Portland, OR; PHOTO: Roger Turk/Northlight Photography; **#3** DESIGN: Steven M. Foote, FAIA, Perry Dean Rogers & Partners, Boston, MA; PHOTO: Brian Vanden Brink; **#4** PHOTO: David Duncan Livingston; **#5** DESIGN: Scogin Elam & Bray Architects, Atlanta, GA; PHOTO: Brian Vanden Brink; **#6** PHOTO: Brian Vanden Brink

pp. 104-105 **#1** DESIGN: James Gillan; PHOTO: David Duncan Livingston; **#2** DESIGN: Miller Dolezal Group, Woodside, CA; PHOTO: David Duncan Livingston; **#3** DESIGN: Scott Johnson/Johnson Fain Partners, Los Angeles, CA; PHOTO: Tim Street-Porter; **#4** DESIGN: Victoria Holland, Bellevue, WA; PHOTO: Andrew Wormer/*Fine Homebuilding* magazine, ©The Taunton Press; **#5** DESIGN: Backen, Arrigoni & Ross, San Francisco, CA; PHOTO: David Duncan Livingston

pp. 106-107 **#1** PHOTO: courtesy Absolute by American Standard; **#2** DESIGN: Delores Hyden, CKD, CBD, Showplace Design & Remodeling, Redmond, WA; PHOTO: Roger Turk/Northlight Photography; **#3** PHOTO: courtesy Kohler; **#4** PHOTO: courtesy Image/PS Craftsmanship; **#5** DESIGN: Carole Katleman Interiors, Beverly Hills, CA; SINK: Farnese Gallery, Los Angeles, CA; PHOTO: Tim Street-Porter

pp. 108-109 **#1** PHOTO: Jeremy Samuelson; **#2** DESIGN: Kitchens & More, San Rafael, CA; PHOTO: David Duncan Livingston; **#3** DESIGN: Steven Erhlich; PHOTO: Grey Crawford; **#4** DESIGN: Brad Rabinowitz, Burlington, VT; PHOTO: Carolyn L. Bates; **#5** PHOTO: Tim Street-Porter

pp. 110-111 **#1** PHOTO: David Duncan Livingston; **#2** PHOTO: courtesy Kohler; **#3** DESIGN: Osburn Design, San Francisco, CA; PHOTO: David Duncan Livingston; **#4** PHOTO: David Duncan Livingston; **#5** PHOTO: courtesy Moen; **#6** PHOTO: courtesy Kohler; **#7** PHOTO: courtesy Delta Select

pp. 112-113 **#1** DESIGN: Lesley Harris; PHOTO: Tim Street-Porter; **#2** PHOTO: David Duncan Livingston; **#3** PHOTO: courtesy Kohler; **#4** DESIGN: Robert Nebulon, Berkeley, CA; PHOTO: David Duncan Livingston; **#5** DESIGN: Brian A. Murphy, BAM Construction/Design, Inc., Santa Monica, CA; PHOTO: Tim Street-Porter; **#6** PHOTO: courtesy Kohler; **#7** PHOTO: courtesy Porcher; **#8** PHOTO: David Duncan Livingston

pp. 114-115 **#1** DESIGN: Suzanne Tucker, Tucker & Marks, San Francisco, CA PHOTO: Tim Street-Porter; **#2** PHOTO: courtesy Gerber; **#3** PHOTO: courtesy Moen; **#4** DESIGN: Osburn Design, San Francisco, CA; PHOTO: David Duncan Livingston; **#5** DESIGN: James F. Vivrette/Altera Design & Remodeling, Orinda, CA PHOTO: David Duncan Livingston

STORAGE SOLUTIONS

pp. 116-117 DESIGN: Hilary Newberry Interior Design, Redmond, WA, and Insiah Libman/Threshold Interior Design, Kirkland, WA; PHOTO: Roger Turk/Northlight Photography

pp. 118-119 **#1** PHOTO: David Duncan Livingston; **#2** PHOTO: David Duncan Livingston; **#3** DESIGN: Vermont Vernacular Designs, East Calais, VT; PHOTO: Carolyn L. Bates; **#4** DESIGN: Suzanne Tucker, Tucker & Marks, San Francisco, CA, G. C. Forde Mazzola Associates, San Francisco, CA; PHOTO: Tim Street-Porter

pp. 120-121 **#1** PHOTO: David Duncan Livingston; **#2** PHOTO: David Duncan Livingston; **#3** DESIGN: John Brenneis Architects, Seattle, WA; PHOTO: Roger Turk/Northlight Photography; **#4** DESIGN: Bill Lane, Los Angeles, CA; PHOTO: Tim Street-Porter

pp. 122-123 **#1** DESIGN: Julie Atwood, Glen Ellen, CA; PHOTO: David Duncan Livingston; **#2** DESIGN: Michael Berman, Los Angeles, CA; PHOTO: Grey Crawford; **#3** PHOTO: courtesy Toto USA; **#4** DESIGN: Richard's Kitchen & Bath Center, Muncie, IN; PHOTO: David Duncan Livingston

pp. 124-125 **#1** DESIGN: Janice Stone Thomas, ASID, CKD/Stonewood Design, Inc., Sacramento, CA; PHOTO: David Duncan Livingston; **#2** DESIGN: Lisa Bonneville, ASID, Bonneville Design, Manchester-by-the-Sea, MA; PHOTO: Steve Vierra; **#3** DESIGN: Sant Architects, Inc., Venice, CA; PHOTO: Grey Crawford; **#4** DESIGN: MB Cushman Design Inc., Stowe, VT; PHOTO: Carolyn L. Bates

pp. 126-127 **#1** DESIGN: Rob Quigley, San Diego, CA; PHOTO: Tim Street Porter; **#2** DESIGN: Jim Rozanski, Issaquah, WA; PHOTO: Roger Turk/Northlight Photography; **#3** DESIGN: Lynn Williams Interiors, Charlotte, VT; PHOTO: Carolyn L. Bates; **#4** DESIGN: Lamperti Associates, San Rafael, CA; PHOTO: David Duncan Livingston; **#5** PHOTO: David Duncan Livingston; **#6** DESIGN: Jackie Goedde/JG Design, CKD, CBD, Seattle, WA; PHOTO: Mark Frey

pp. 128-129 **#1** DESIGN: Paul Egee; CONSTRUCTION: Stephen Tobin; PHOTO: Kevin Ireton/*Fine Homebuilding* magazine, ©The Taunton Press; **#2** PHOTO: Jeremy Samuelson; **#3** PHOTO: Malcolm Appleton; STYLING: Barbara Stratton; PHOTO: Carolyn L. Bates; **#4** PHOTO: Jeremy Samuelson; **#5** DESIGN: Richard's Kitchen & Bath Center, Muncie, IN; PHOTO: David Duncan Livingston

pp. 130-131 **#1** PHOTO: Jeremy Samuelson; **#2** DESIGN: John Anderson; PHOTO: Steve Culpepper/*Fine Homebuilding* magazine, ©The Taunton Press; **#3** PHOTO: Steve Vierra; **#4** DESIGN: Paul Egee; PHOTO: Kevin Ireton/*Fine Homebuilding* magazine, ©The Taunton Press; **#5** PHOTO: Jeremy Samuelson; **#6** DESIGN: Fro Vakili/Brian A. Murphy, BAM Construction/Design, Inc., Santa Monica, CA; PHOTO: Tim Street-Porter

pp. 132-133 **#1** DESIGN: MB Cushman Design, Inc., Stowe, VT; PHOTO: Carolyn L. Bates; **#2** PHOTO: Grey Crawford; **#3** DESIGN: Julie Wright Interior Design, Corte Madera, CA; PHOTO: David Duncan Livingston; **#4** DESIGN: Siri Evju/Neil Kelly Designers & Remodelers, Portland, OR; PHOTO: David Duncan Livingston; **#5** DESIGN: Susan Greischel, San Francisco, CA; PHOTO: David Duncan Livingston

pp. 134-135 **#1** DESIGN: Osburn Design, San Francisco, CA; PHOTO: David Duncan Livingston **#2** DESIGN: Joszi Meskan, San Francisco, CA; PHOTO: David Duncan Livingston; **#3** DESIGN: Fu Tung Cheng; PHOTO: Jeremy Samuelson

pp. 136-137 **#1** PHOTO: Grey Crawford; **#2** DESIGN: Peggy Deras, CKD, CID, Kitchen Artworks, South San Francisco, CA; PHOTO: David Duncan Livingston; **#3** DESIGN: Martha Kerr, Neil Kelly Designers/Remodelers, Portland, OR; PHOTO: David Duncan Livingston; **#4** DESIGN: Acorn Kitchen and Bath, Oakland, CA; PHOTO: David Duncan Livingston; **#5** PHOTO: David Duncan Livingston; **#6** DESIGN: Gerard Ciccarello, CKD, CBD/Covenant Kitchens and Baths, Westbrook, CT; PHOTO: Jim Fiora

LIGHTING, HEATING, AND VENTILATION

pp. 138-139 DESIGN: Nick Berman Design, Los Angeles, CA; PHOTO: Grey Crawford

pp. 140-141 **#1** DESIGN: Albee O'Hara, Inc., South Royalton, VT; PHOTO: Carolyn L. Bates; **#2** PHOTO: Jonathan Hillyer, courtesy Toto; **#3** DESIGN: Stephen G. Smith Architects, Camden, ME; PHOTO: Brian Vanden Brink; **#4** DESIGN: Osburn Design, San Francisco, CA; PHOTO: David Duncan Livingston; **#5** DESIGN: Michael Guthrie, San Francisco, CA; PHOTO: David Duncan Livingston; **#6** DESIGN: Gary White, CID, CKD, CBD, Kitchen & Bath Design, Newport Beach, CA; PHOTO: Larry Falke pp. 142-143 #1 DESIGN: Richard Fearn; PHOTO: *Fine Homebuilding* magazine, ©The Taunton Press; #2 DESIGN: Tom Cabot; Shelburne, VT; PHOTO: Carolyn L. Bates; #3 DESIGN: Martha Kerr, Neil Kelly Designers/Remodelers, Portland, OR; PHOTO: David Duncan Livingston; #4 DESIGN: GKW Working Design; PHOTO: Carolyn L. Bates; #5 DESIGN: Stephen G. Smith Architects, Camden, ME; PHOTO: Brian Vanden Brink

pp. 144-145 #1 PHOTO: Grey Crawford; #2 DESIGN: Richard Rouilard; PHOTO: Tim Street-Porter; #3 DESIGN: Elliott & Elliott Architecture, Blue Hill, ME; LIGHTING DESIGN: Peter Knuppel, Gouldsboro, ME; PHOTO: Brian Vanden Brink

pp. 146-147 #1 DESIGN: Chris Campbell, Chris Campbell Design, Jefferson, ME; PHOTO: Brian Vanden Brink; #2 DESIGN: Frank K. Pennino & Associates, Los Angeles, CA; PHOTO: Tim Street-Porter; #3 DESIGN: Judith R. Bracht, Tunis Kitchen and Bath, Chevy Chase, MD; PHOTO: Peter Margonelli, NKBA; #4 DESIGN: Tom Trzcinski, Pittsburgh, PA; PHOTO: Maura McEvoy, NKBA; #5 PHOTO: Brian Vanden Brink

pp. 148-149 #1 DESIGN: John Morris Architects, Camden, ME; PHOTO: Brian Vanden Brink; #2 DESIGN: Martha Kerr, Neil Kelly Designers/ Remodelers, Portland, OR; PHOTO: David Duncan Livingston; #3 PHOTO: Carolyn L. Bates; #4 DESIGN: Michael Dugan; PHOTO: courtesy Broan; #5 PHOTO: Brian Vanden Brink

pp. 150-151 #1 DESIGN: Ted Montgomery/ Indiana Architecture & Design, Charlotte, VT; TOWEL WARMER: Myson; PHOTO: Carolyn L. Bates; #2 PHOTO: courtesy Runtal North America; #3 DESIGN: Michael Dugan; PHOTO: Carolyn L. Bates; #4 PHOTO: Brian Vanden Brink; #5 DESIGN: MB Cushman Design, Inc., Stowe, VT; PHOTO: Carolyn L. Bates

BEYOND THE BASIC BATH

pp. 152-153 DESIGN: MB Cushman Design, Inc., Stowe, VT; PHOTO: Carolyn L. Bates

pp. 154-155 #1 PHOTO: courtesy Finnleo; #2 DESIGN: David Coleman/Architecture, Seattle, WA; PHOTO: Carolyn L. Bates; #3 DESIGN: Centerbrook Architects and Planners, Centerbrook, CT; PHOTO: Brian Vanden Brink

pp. 156-157 #1 DESIGN: MB Cushman Design, Inc., Stowe, VT; PHOTO: Carolyn L. Bates; #2 PHOTO: courtesy Bisazza; #3 DESIGN: David Coleman, Seattle, WA; PHOTOS: Carolyn L. Bates; #4 PHOTO: Carolyn L. Bates

pp. 158-159 #1 PHOTO: Tim Street-Porter; #2 DESIGN: David Lawrence Gray Architects, AIA, Santa Monica, CA; PHOTO: Tim Street-Porter; #3 DESIGN: Brian A. Murphy, BAM Construction/ Design, Inc., Santa Monica, CA; CUBICLE CONSTRUCTION: Simon Maltby; PHOTO: Tim Street-Porter; #4 DESIGN: Holden & Dupuy, New Orleans, LA; PHOTO: Tim Street-Porter; #5 DESIGN: Russ Leland, Los Angeles, CA; PHOTO: Tim Street-Porter; #6 PHOTO: Tim Street-Porter

pp. 160-161 #1 DESIGN: Brian A. Murphy, BAM Construction/Design, Inc., Santa Monica, CA; TUB CONSTRUCTION: Simon Maltby; PHOTO: Tim Street-Porter; #2 DESIGN: Tom Catalano, Catalano Architects and Catalano Design, Boston, MA; PHOTO: Brian Vanden Brink; #3 DESIGN: Suzanne Tucker, Tucker & Marks, San Francisco, CA; PHOTO: Tim Street-Porter

pp. 162-163 #1 DESIGN: Molly Korb, CKD, CBD, MK Designs, Newcastle, CA/Linda Panattoni, Panattoni Interiors, Sacramento, CA; PHOTOS: David Duncan Livingston, NKBA; #2 PHOTO: Tim Street-Porter; #3 PHOTO: courtesy Kohler; #4 PHOTO: courtesy Kohler

PUBLISHER

JIM CHILDS

ACQUISITIONS EDITOR

STEVE CULPEPPER

EDITORIAL ASSISTANT

CAROL KASPER

COPY EDITOR

PETER CHAPMAN

DESIGNER/LAYOUT ARTIST

HENRY ROTH

ILLUSTRATOR

JOANNE KELLAR BOUKNIGHT